God's Will is to Do it For You

God's Will is to Do it For You

*If it's not Total Victory, Total Success
Then it's Not God's Will for Your Life*

Robbie Albrighton

Copyright © 2020 by Robbie Albrighton.

ISBN-978-1-6485-8115-1

All rights reserved. No part of this book may be reproduced or transmitted in any form or by any means, electronic or mechanical, including photocopying, recording, or by any information storage and retrieval system, without permission in writing from the copyright owner.

The views expressed in this work are solely those of the author and do not necessarily reflect the views of the publisher, and the publisher hereby disclaims any responsibility for them.

Matchstick Literary
1-888-306-8885
orders@matchliterary.com

Contents

Introduction ix

Chapter 1	"I Do Not Think God Would Give Me Anything"...	1
Chapter 2	God is Not Moved by your Troubles	4
Chapter 3	Lord Increase our Faith The Secret of Releasing.................................	12
Chapter 4	Receiving In His Name It's Free It Works and it is The Will of God.............	18
Chapter 5	If God Be For Us Who Can Be Against Us? Your Enemy that's Who!	22
Chapter 6	Faith the Invisible Force? So What is it Exactly?................................	27
Chapter 7	The Honesty and Integrity of God's Word	52
Chapter 8	Your Inner Image of Yourself. Creates Your Future	62
Chapter 9	Be led By the Holy Spirit................................	73
Chapter 10	Grace to Help	89
Chapter 11	First the Blade The Law of Patient Progression	93
Chapter 12	Healing God Wants You Well................................	103
Chapter 13	The Ministry of Angels	137
Chapter 14	The Names reflect the Nature of God	148
Chapter 15	What Happens at "The End"	153

Conclusion 175
Bibliography 177

THIS BOOK IS DEDICATED TO
THE MINISTRY OF KEN AND GLORIA COPELAND
WHOS FAITHFUL SERVICE TO GOD CAUSED ME
TO KNOW THE THINGS THAT
HAVE LED TO A JOURNEY
OF FAITH AND ACCOMPLISHMENT THAT
ISN'T OVER YET

AND TO MY DARLING WIFE CAROL
WHO INSPIRES ME TO BE ALL THAT
I CAN BE IN GOD, AND MAKES ME
WANT TO ACHIEVE GREAT THINGS.
AND FOR HER EDITING TIME

Introduction

THE PURPOSE OF this book is to educate and to encourage. If by reading this book you are inspired to believe God and press in for a more abundant healthier more exciting life; feeling that you can at last achieve great things in God because He loves you and will keep His word to you then I have achieved what I set out to do.

There are a lot of topics mentioned in this book sometimes more than one is touched on under a particular heading and so is by no means intended to be an in-depth study of any of the subjects. They are approached with more of an over view attitude with commentary and testimony relative to what I considered to be the basic understanding needed to succeed in the particular area discussed.

At the time of writing this book I have been ministering to people in one form or another for thirty five years and for thirty five years I've watched people who love God die sick, go broke and sometimes just give up through circumstances that at the time seem to be well and truly out of their control. It breaks my heart to see people who love God and those that don't know Him, both struggling and being torn apart by the situations they are facing, while all the time knowing that in the Word of God lies the answer if they only realized and believed it.

God has always intended for mankind to live as the Jewel in the crown of His creation. He never at any stage intended man to be subject to sickness, disease, poverty, pain, worry or even death. These things have come on us as a course of events outside the will of God's intention. So as a consequence of the pressures of this life God has been given the reputation of one who brings or allows suffering or at best just doesn't do anything about it, and that's simply not true. **God's will is to do it for you,** so hopefully these pages will go some way to correcting that thinking in all who read them.

God bless you and may He quicken His Word to your Hearts and minds as you read this book. Love to you and yours in Jesus name *Robbie Albrighton.* ☺

Chapter One

"I Do Not Think God Would Give Me Anything"

> 7. "……Verily, verily, I say unto you, whatsoever ye shall ask the Father in my name, he will give it to you." (Jn.15 v 7)

THIS VERSE MAY seem like a pretty bold statement to make or believe, some may even say ridiculous, there may even be those who feel totally justified in saying that it's just downright presumptuous that the person that would, or feels that they could receive on the basis of a statement like that in all good conscience, must be suffering from either a really bad case of spiritual pride or they are simply deluded. (Even though I think that is exactly what God wants us to do.)

Well I dare say that there would be many who agree with them, some because they genuinely don't believe such a thing, based on their particular religious denomination's teachings and those that simply find the prospect of that statement too big a promise in terms of what they consider they deserve. Again though it may well come back to what is taught in their particular denomination in terms of being deserving.

If there is one thing that I have seen in over thirty years of Sharing God's Word that is evident time and time again, it is that people just can't believe that God would do the things they ask of Him. They know God can do it after all He is God; and they believe that He might do it for someone like the Pastor or a person they believe is good and continually working for God in some area, they would like to receive from God they want to believe it could happen, but they just can't believe that God would do it for them personally right now just because they asked Him to. This is a great shame and must grieve the Spirit of God continually to think that His children believe that He doesn't think enough of a particular individual to move on their behalf. The Bible says that "if we being evil know how to give good things to our children then how much more would God who is your loving Heavenly Father give good things to you." **(Matt. 7 v 11)**

Well let's have a look at what the Word of God says; firstly we read where the scripture said that what we asked in His name (Jesus') God would give us. The reason Jesus made that statement with confidence is that He knew that when God looks at us who is asking He doesn't see our faults and weaknesses as we do but he sees us through the Blood of Jesus shed for us on the cross; paying the price for our sins and so paving the way, giving us the right, becoming our substitute for punishment and cursing so that we can now approach God with a clean slate. The Bible says that He has forgiven us all our trespasses;

> **14. "blotting out the hand writing of ordinances that was against us, and took it out of the way nailing it to his cross." (Col. 2 v 14)**

In other words all the laws of do's and don'ts that we've all broken and all the things that religion still tells us we're either going to hell for or that simply make us ineligible to receive have been paid for by the blood that was shed on the cross at Calvary, making it possible for us to come to God and ask anything of Him without fear of rejection. The only thing He can't do for us is to believe Him.

> **"Let us therefore come boldly unto the throne of grace that we may obtain mercy, and find grace to help in time of need." (Heb. 4 v 16)**

What a wonderful promise that is. What a great privilege to be able to walk up to God as your loving Father and ask for what you need without feeling inadequate or unworthy. Jesus himself referred to God as your Father. The Bible says that;

> **"Behold what manner of love the Father hath bestowed upon us, that we should be called the sons of God; therefore the world knoweth us not, because it knoweth him not." (Jn. 3 v 10)**

Too many people see God as a task Master or a Boss figure. Some even see Him as someone to be feared because they think that He puts sickness on them or has storms blow their houses away, in what's called *"acts of God"*. They're not acts of God, He's the life giver not the taker, the Bible says that God is love. You do have an enemy that seeks to kill steal and destroy **(Jn. 10 v 10**) but it isn't God. We'll uncover who he is and how he operates a little later.

When the Bible talks of fearing God it doesn't mean afraid, it means respect. Wrong teaching has created wrong believing over the years; the Bible says that God is happy about you doing well and wants to help you achieve good things in your life and that God has pleasure in the prosperity of His servant **(Pslm.35 v 27**). Jesus went as far as to say that it is your father's good pleasure to give you the Kingdom **(Lk. 12 v 32)** and if the Kingdom then that means all that it's made up of such as Eternal Life, Prosperity, Peace, Joy, Healing, Guidance and Counsel, God has the Bible says, given to us all that pertains to life and Godliness through the knowledge of Him that has called us to glory and virtue. **(2Pet. 1 v 3)** Hallelujah everything that is relevant to life and Godliness, well that covers everything spiritually, mentally, physically, financially and socially, every area of human existence, so why do so many people struggle through life barely getting their needs met when **God's will is to do it for you?**

The secret is in the fact that your circumstances don't move God, He is concerned and cares for you and wants to help, but the situation is not what causes God to do anything on your behalf. So what does?

Chapter Two

God is Not Moved by your Troubles

WELL WHAT KIND of statement is that you ask? First you tell me that God wants to do things for me, then, you say He's not moved by my troubles. Well what is He moved by?

A lot of us have different views about what God will do, can do and how these things come about, and who they'll be done for. I used to think that if I could ever be good enough for long enough, God might do something for me, but deep down I never felt that I would really make the grade, after all God sees everything, and I had stuff in my life that wasn't so great. Then I had some teaching that began to change my way of thinking. In the **eleventh chapter of Mark** Jesus said that;

> "For verily I say unto you, that whosoever shall say unto this mountain, be thou removed and be thou cast into the sea; and shall not doubt in his heart, but shall believe that those things which he saith shall come to pass; he shall have whatsoever he saith." (Mk. 11 v 23)

Notice that Jesus said whosoever, well who is whosoever? I read the words but my thinking was always that "whosoever" was someone good, better than I was. I didn't know exactly who I was thinking of, but it never felt as though it was talking about me. The word whosoever though means just that, anyone. Well if God says that anybody can have the things that they ask then it must be based on something other than good works, because I didn't feel that I was personally doing many.

Let's look at Hebrews chapter eleven verse six,

> "But without faith it is impossible to please him; for he that cometh to God must believe that he is, and that he is a rewarder of them that diligently seek him."

Notice that it says we must believe that He will reward us. The key is to believe that He will reward us when we come to Him. Many people love God and believe that God loves them, but they somehow put receiving from Him into another category in their thinking. We do this because we believe deep down that we are not deserving and not worthy to receive any great thing from God; but thanks be to God who, because of His great love for us, sent His Son to make our righteousness of Him.

> "But of him are ye in Christ Jesus, who of God is made unto us wisdom, and righteousness, and sanctification, and redemption;" (1Cor. 1 v 30)

> "For He hath made him to be sin for us, who knew no sin; that we might be made the righteousness of God in him." (11 Cor. 5 v 21)

We don't come to God on the basis of our righteousness we come on the basis of Christ Jesus' righteousness. Even though we've heard the words many times people still cringe if you ask them are they righteous? But it's precisely this right standing with God through Jesus that qualifies us to receive from Him.

When my Children's Mother was younger before we were married, she had an operation for a condition called endometriosis, where the ovaries and tubes become entangled in fibrous tissue resulting in very painful period time and difficulty in conceiving a child. After the procedure the Surgeon told her that she would not be able to conceive a child naturally and a very slim chance even on the Invitro plan because of the amount of scaring, due to the fact they had to remove her ovaries and tubes during the operation.

This was heart breaking for her, and for a long time she believed that children of her own were not hers to hope for. God on the other hand said in **Marks Gospel** that whosoever; and we were whosoever's, so we put our faith in God to keep His word; and having filled our hearts with His promises and meditated on the Word which told us that He loved us, we began to believe that it would happen for us.

We put our petition before Him on the basis of His word, and He told me what to say and how to believe Him in this. Then God gave us two beautiful girls conceived and born naturally over the next few years, praise God His Word is settled in heaven forever the Bible said. A lot of people still had a problem with what they called our Hyper Faith doctrine, but you see it wasn't our doctrine, it is God's doctrine, He wrote the Bible not us. In the **twenty forth verse of Marks Gospel**, right after the words, whosoever can say, it says this;

> **"Therefore (or because of this promise) I say unto you, that what things so ever ye desire, when ye pray, believe that ye receive them, and ye shall have them." (Mk. 11 v 24)**

Well we desired to have children and God gave us the desire of our hearts. He is a good and loving father. You see it wasn't our circumstances that moved God, it was our faith in His Word, having faith that He would do that which He said He would for whoever asked Him, and kept on believing until it came into being. A lot of people still felt somehow even though we had received from God that we were being spiritually proud, or taking God for granted, and using Him, as one person put it, *"you can't just use God like a lolly shop."* This comes from someone who can't, through a lack of faith, receive from God and so becomes offended at the testimony of another.

Most people however were thrilled for us and praised God for doing a miracle for us and for his goodness. There were times when doubt tried to creep in, like the day my wife's period started, and the devil said to her, "you can't be pregnant if you have your period can you"? It reminded me of the serpent in the Garden of Eden saying to Eve that surely you wouldn't die if you eat from the tree of knowledge of good and evil, you see your enemy the devil always wants to tempt you into thinking God didn't really mean what He said. Yes there were opportunities to fear and doubt but we simply said no, God is faithful who promised, and the issue stopped and the child was manifest.

Jesus said in the fourteenth chapter of John that;

> **"If you ask anything in my name**
> **I will do it" (Jn. 14v14).**

I simply choose to believe that God means what He says. Now we'll have debate among people in regard to Logos and Rhema Word, in other words taking the general Word of God as literal, or getting a special word on a subject from God before it will work. My personal thought is how many times does He have to say it? There are times when a Word is for you at a specific time, but you don't need a special word to believe to receive something Jesus bought for you on the cross. Well Jesus said according to your faith be it unto you **(Matt. 9 v 29)** so I'll leave that one to the individual but I'll keep telling you as I believe things to be. What I do know is this, **Romans chapter ten verses nine and ten** tell us;

> **9. "That if you shalt confess with thy**
> **mouth the Lord Jesus, and shalt believe**
> **in thine heart that God has raised him**
> **from the dead, thou shalt be saved."**

> **10. "For with the heart man believes**
> **unto righteousness; and with the mouth**
> **confession is made unto salvation."**

What this tells me, is that God's way is to believe for something and then confess it as so, believe Jesus is Lord then say He is my savior, believe I can have a child and confess that they are here, believe that I am healed and then say I'm well in Jesus name. The principal is the same and that's God's way of operating with us, He tells us what is available to us and then when we believe for it and speak it out, He manifests it for us in the earth. Now a lot of people will say, "Oh yes, but we have to ask according to His will before He will give it to you and what you are asking for may not be His will for you". Ok let's look what the Bible says about it. You see it doesn't matter what I think and it doesn't matter what someone else thinks, if it's not what God thinks it doesn't amount to any good at all, and there will be no power to perform or create anything.

The scriptures tell us that;

> **14 "And this is the confidence that we have in him that if we ask anything according to his will, he heareth us."**
>
> **15 "And if we know that he hears us, whatsoever we ask, we know that we have the petitions that we desired of him."**

Ok the scripture clearly says that if He hears us we know He will grant us our petitions. The prerequisite here is that to be heard we must ask in line with his will. Well let's look at the will of God from the Word. You see God gave us the Word to clear up our thinking, to get us thinking the right way so He could fellowship with us, give us things, and generally have a good time with His family. A lot of people still have trouble believing that God actually likes us, let alone wants to hang around with us. That's a shame and these people have obviously not understood the relationship that God wants for us and Him together. A good way to understand this is to spend time with God, prayer is one way, another is to get involved in believing for something like your healing, it will cause you to read scripture and know His presence while you persevere for the result. At the end of it you'll know more and understand your Father all the better.

If someone says their will is for you to have something you wanted for Christmas, and that something you desired was a watch, their will is to get you what you wanted, so they would buy you a watch. When they gave you the present you would be grateful and over joyed to receive the gift, but not surprised at their choice, because they told you they wished to give you what you wanted. They would have in buying the gift, accomplished what they wanted to do, which was to buy you what you chose. In other words their will was to do what you had asked them for; so then their will was your will. Now let's see that same principal in the Word and see if it applies to God.

Again let's look to **Mark chapter eleven verse twenty four** where Jesus say's

> **"Therefore I say unto you, what things soever ye desire, when ye pray, believe that ye receive them and ye shall have them." (Mk.11 v 24)**

We see here that God is saying what things that you desire, the things that you want, the things that you are praying for, so your will in the matter is now God's will in the matter. To say anything else in relation to this verse would be to say to God that He is not telling the truth. You would have to say He is lying because He said, what you want is what I will do. Therefore that's His will on the matter.

It seems silly to the converted mind that God would send Jesus to die for us who deserved nothing, give up His only son unto death, (and that's not something a parent would enjoy), have Jesus bare our grief, our poverty, our sickness and diseases and all of our sins, in fact the sins of the whole world past present and future, and then go to the trouble of having the Bible promises put into print, not to mention all that the Disciples and Paul went through, just to turn around and say "No you can't be healed of that cough or you can't have your needs met because that's too much to ask for". It sounds silly doesn't it, but that's the kind of thinking that people must be getting into somehow, by thinking that God wouldn't give to them what they ask. It would be like someone buying you a Qantas A380 Jet for Christmas, and then saying you can't have a seat cover for the Pilot's seat because it costs too much.

When Blind Bartimaeus called out to Jesus the Lord asked him; **"What wilt thou that I should do unto thee?"** And he said he wanted to be able to see. Jesus didn't say "now wait a minute that may not be God's will" He didn't say "who do you think you are asking for such a gift"? No He just healed him. **(Mk.10 v 46-52)** You see Jesus' will was God's will. He said, "I only do what the Father tells me and He said to Bartimaeus, "what will you have me do for you"? So now that means God's will was to fulfill Bartimaeus' will. Here again is the will of God shown to be as Jesus said,

> 24. "What things soever you desire......." (Mk. 11v 4) All throughout the New Testament we can see God's willingness to bless His people in **Johns Gospel chapter fifteen verse seven** we read;

> 7. "If you abide in me, and my words abide in you, ye shall ask what ye will, and it shall be done unto you." (Jn. 15v7).

Now some may be thinking that Jesus only meant these promises to be for the Disciples, just for the special twelve and if so, it would be impossible for things to happen for us. But the Bible tells us in the book of **Acts in the tenth chapter and the thirty forth verse** this;
Then Peter opened his mouth, and said,

> 34. "Of a truth I perceive that God is no respecter of persons." (Acts 10v34).

What this means to you and I is that If God would do something for Peter or Paul or Mark etc He is bound by His own Word to do it for everybody that will believe Him for it and that's not a problem for God, He wants us to have our needs met it's His Idea. In Philippians the Bible tells us;

> "But my God shall supply all your need according to his riches in glory by Christ Jesus." (9 Phil. 4 v 19)

Again let me remind you that the blessings that are ours in God are not ours based on our righteousness, but on the righteousness of Jesus the Christ. So God meeting your needs is because of Jesus' sacrifice and because He is in Heaven interceding for us continually; and that makes it easier to believe. God is doing it for us because Jesus wants Him to, He paid for the privilege of us having our needs met. **God's will is to do it for us**.

Ok we've seen that God wants us to have things and that He wants to do what we ask, so then if we are eligible, and He's willing, why then is it so hard sometimes, why does it seem so often that we don't have enough faith to make things work for us, or enough faith to get God to move on our behalf?

There's an old joke about a farmer who was clearing trees on his property, one day when his old trusty axe broke. He went into his local grower's hardware and asked the assistant for a new axe. The assistant said to the old farmer "why don't you take this chainsaw instead it will make life a lot easier for you". The old farmer said "ok" and took the chainsaw home. A couple of weeks later the old farmer was back complaining of a sore back and tired arms and the fact that he was better off with his old axe as this new fangled thing just isn't as good. The assistant said "that can't be right there must be something wrong it must be blunt or something. I'll check it and sharpen the chain for you". The old farmer agreed and the assistant turned on the fuel, primed the fuel ball and pulled the chord. The chainsaw roared into life and the old farmer jumped backwards and shouted "what the hell is that noise"? You see sometimes there is something we don't know and that can make all the difference.

Chapter Three

Lord Increase our Faith
The Secret of Releasing

> 5. "And the Apostles said unto the Lord, increase our faith."
>
> 6. "And the Lord said, If ye had faith as a grain of mustard seed, ye might say unto this Sycamine tree, Be thou plucked up by the root, and be thou planted in the sea; and it should obey you." (Lk. 17 v 5-6)

A LOT OF the time people say to me, as did the Apostles to Jesus, that they wish they had more faith, or that they had the faith that I have because they know of the things that have happened for me of the Lord.

I was praying for people one time during a Friday night service. We'd had a good meeting, the anointing was in the room and I asked for people that wanted prayer to come forward. I particularly asked a person with Arthritis that the Lord had told me was in the meeting to come forward, because God knew of her condition and wanted to heal her. In fact I called her forward before anyone else but no one came forward. I told the congregation that it was ok if the person chose not to come forward because it was her choice, and I was confident that I was right in what I had heard. As the people were invited to come, I began to pray, and God was healing and sorting out various conditions. A lady came forward with what she called a bleeding Hernia.

She had not been able to eat for fear of choking on her food and had to sleep sitting up. I began to pray and she joined her faith with mine, and God moved and healed her on the spot. She said the pain had left her and she felt in herself that she was healed. Laura, as I will call her told us the following week that she went home and ate a steak for supper, then laid down flat and had a good night's sleep.

The following week she came forward and gave testimony to the healing power of the prayer, and the goodness of God. Apparently God not only healed her of the Hernia but at breakfast the next morning, being overjoyed at the fact that she was healed, was giving thanks to God and singing Him praise. At that point her fingers, which had the arthritic condition that I had called her out for the night that she had been healed of her other condition, suddenly began to heal and her fingers began to crack and become straight. She showed us during the service the following week her beautiful straight fingers which had no sign of any arthritic condition, and were not painful. Of course we were all excited about what God was doing in our midst.

What gives some people the power to receive miracles? And others seem to get nothing when they know they love God and often are called to minister in His name. The secret is in the scripture we started this chapter with, so let's look at it, and the following four verses, as Jesus teaches the Apostles the truth hidden for us in the scriptures.

Jesus begins to teach us by saying;

> If you had faith as a grain of mustard seed, you might say to the tree be plucked up etc. Notice here He says,
>
> AS A GRAIN of mustard seed not, if you had faith the SIZE of a mustard seed. Here He is not teaching about how much faith you have, but how you use your faith. The Apostles thought they needed more faith but Jesus said, they need to plant, or use their faith as the seed, so it can work or produce for them, and He is about to show them how to use that which they already had.

In the following verses **seven eight nine and ten** Jesus begins to relate the principle operation of a servant, how he serves you, and when you are served, then he may eat himself. The thing Jesus was trying to get across to the Disciples is that your faith is given to you to work for you as would a servant. He was explaining to them that they should have the expectation that their faith would work for them, serve them and create for them, just as surely as would a servant who was living in their home.

> **7. "But which of you, Having a servant plowing or feeding cattle, will say unto him by and by, when he is come from the field, Go and sit down to meat." (Lk. 17v7)**

Jesus is saying that for you to say to a servant sit down to food I've made for you is an unrealistic expectation on his part. No, he serves you first and then he may eat, he is there to serve your needs that's his purpose in life.

> **8. "And will not rather say unto him, Make ready where with I may sup, and gird thyself, and serve me, till I have eaten and drunken; and afterward thou shall eat and drink?" (Lk. 17v8)**

He then goes on to say;

> **9. "Doth he thank that servant that servant because he did the things that were commanded of him? I trow not." (Lk. 17v9)**

You see the master doesn't thank a servant for doing the thing that he is hired to do, or is paid to do. It's a reasonable thing to expect that your orders will be carried out, yes? The very fact that Jesus uses such an example as a servant is a clear indication that faith is meant to serve you faithfully and without exception. In other words He is saying to us don't be surprised that your faith will produce what you speak, because that's what it's for, to serve you as a servant does his master. Jesus is showing them that they don't need more faith they need to exercise, or release the faith they already had, and we know they had faith because Jesus had been teaching them. Faith comes by hearing the Word and Jesus is the Word.

And the Bible says in the book of Romans that,

> **17. "So then faith cometh by hearing and hearing by the Word of God." (Rom. 10 v 17).**

So they had heard the Word of God from Jesus, so with their hearing faith would be present in them, and He had explained to them that they should expect it to work for them.

People I teach often find the concept that faith is something we can use as we would a tool or a power unit or even a person quite presumptuous. I think a lot of people just think of faith as some mystical power that old prophets or super spiritual Evangelists posses like a magic wand or cape of distinction. Some just use it as an expression of their believing in God as, being in the faith.

If you will accept what Jesus is teaching in these scriptures, and that is that your faith will work for you and create and produce things and situations for you in your lives, then we need to see just how to make it work for us.

Let's look at the scripture we saw earlier from the **eleventh chapter of Marks Gospel**. We looked at this scripture in relation to whosoever, now I want us to look at it in relation to releasing our faith. Isn't God wonderful, He has so much truth hidden for us not from us in His Word?

> **23. "For verily I say unto you, That whosoever shall say unto this mountain, be thou removed, and be thou cast into the sea; and shall not doubt in his heart, but shall believe that those things which he saith shall come to pass; he shall have whatsoever he saith."**

Notice how many times the word says or saith is in this scripture. God has ordained that this world is a word ruled planet. He created it with words and the Bible says that He upholds all things by the Word of His Power **(Heb. 1 v 3)** not the power of His Word, this would indicate that there was another recognized power in the universe that had to be understood, no He says the Word of His Power.

He's created with words of faith, (as **Hebrews chapter eleven verse three** tells us), in that God created the worlds by framing the picture of what He wanted to create with His words; and we know from Genesis that He spoke those words out releasing His faith to cause them to come into being as the world and all that's in it we see today, including the heavens above **(Gen. 1 v 26);** and He is showing us here that we can create and cause change to our advantage by releasing our faith in our words, with a believing heart just as God did.

In case you're still a little skeptical about believing that things spoken to the Apostles, or the red writing as it is in some Bibles are for us also, let's see it in the writings of the Apostle Paul written to the Church.

In the book of **Romans** Paul writes in **the fourth chapter seventeenth verse;** speaking of Abraham, who Paul here is encouraging us to follow as an example of faith writes;

> "(As it is written, I have made thee a father of many nations,) before him whom he believed, even God, who quickeneth the dead, and calleth those things which be not as though they were." (Rom. 4 v 17)

Paul is explaining here if you read on that we are to use our words and speak the things we want to come into this world, or into being the way we want them, by calling them done in Jesus name. We always pray and ask in Jesus name, because that's the way God and Jesus both Tell us in the Bible to ask, In His name. Remember He said "ask anything in my name". He is our qualification with God the Father.

This is something else people make a mistake with. The Bible tells us in many places to ask what we will, and to ask in His name, meaning Jesus our Substitute and our redeemer, and God will do it for us. We've looked at some of those scriptures already. For some reason though people still ask in the name of Christ, or in the name of the Father etc. Christ is not Jesus' last name, it means the anointed one, and the one that is anointed is the Word of God, whom Jesus was in the flesh.

This kind of praying sounds religious enough, it sounds all very proper, after all Jesus is the Christ, and God is our Father, but as I said earlier, what you or I or anybody else thinks, if it's not what God says in the Bible it doesn't count for anything. It will not work just because it sounds religious. In fact Jesus said the traditions of men make God's Word ineffective. **(Matt. 15 v 6 and Mk. 7 v 13)** and a lot of our prayers of the past have been in the tradition of the time and prayed as such, to no avail and again people thought that they just didn't have the faith to get answers from God; when they were simply asking the wrong way.

To try and do things the way we think sounds right, instead of how God tells us to, is a form of self righteousness, and not pleasing to God. He has ordained a way for us to receive through the Word based on Jesus' sacrifice and in His name, because **God's will is to do it for you** and that's the way it has to happen.

Chapter Four

Receiving In His Name It's Free It Works and it is The Will of God

THE REASON PRAYING in the name of Jesus is so affective, apart from the fact that God told us to, is because the Bible tells us that God has given Jesus a name above every other name, The Bible tells us in Philippians;

> 9. "Wherefore God hath highly exalted him, and given him a name above every name:"
>
> 10. "That at the name of Jesus every knee should bow, of things in Heaven, and things in Earth, and things under the Earth:"
>
> 11. "And that every tongue should confess that Jesus is Lord, to the Glory of God the Father." (Phil. 2 v 9-11).

What this means to us, is that when we are operating the way God tells us to, in the name of Jesus, that circumstance, sickness, situations involving things we want to change etc, are all things with names, and at the command in the name of Jesus these things etc, must bow their knee. In other words they must submit to the spiritual authority in the Name of Jesus, and become as we want them to be.

Now you might say that's all well and good but I'm not Jesus, and I don't have His name. Well let's see what the Word of God says about it. You see God teaches us about what's ours, about the things He has for us, because like the title of this book says, it's His will to do things for you. He wants people to know how to be saved (be placed in a safe sound position in Christ for eternity), and how to receive and live a happy productive life while we're here on the earth.

Often when speaking to people about receiving Jesus into their lives, they are reluctant to receive Him because they feel they will not be allowed to do the things they like anymore, like drink alcohol, smoke or have money. People have funny ideas about what God expects of them, this too comes from religious teaching that has been handed down through the ages. A lot of it is just simply man made rules to control the lives of parishioners, or just wrong thinking by people who meant well, but didn't really know the heart of God. Like taking a vow of poverty, the Bible says that Jesus our substitute became poor, so we could be made rich **(11Cor. 8 v 9)**.

I think it's enough to say again that Jesus paid for our sins, past present and future on the cross. So you don't miss out on Heaven for what you do, you actually miss out for what you don't do, and that is as **Romans ten verses nine and ten** told us earlier, that we need to believe on Jesus and speak our confession or our belief of the fact, that He is our way to be saved.

God has given us the name of Jesus to use instead of our own name. In this way we face circumstances and situations in His name not ours. It's as though He were standing asking God or giving a command to sickness instead of us. It's called having power of attorney. God has ordained that when we speak in the name of Jesus, He will act as though Jesus Himself is asking.

Jesus said to us;

> 13. "And whatsoever ye shall ask in my name, that will I do, that the Father may be glorified in the Son."

> 14. "If ye shall ask anything in my name, I will do it." (Jn. 14 v 13-14)

He gave us His name to use freely to our advantage. He was given His name by God but He also won His name in combat in hell, by defeating satan our enemy for us, and taking death captive and becoming the Prince of Peace and the Lord of Lords. You may not have thought about it before but we're the kings and lords He's King of Kings and Lord of Lords of. satan's not king or lord of anything, and he never was, he's called and operates as god of this world but it doesn't belong to him. Jesus is the undisputed champion of Heaven, Earth, and Hell, and He stands before us and says;

> 17." And these signs shall follow them that believe; in my name they shall cast out devils; they shall speak with new tongues;"
>
> 18. "They shall take up serpents; and if they drink any deadly thing, it shall not hurt them; they shall lay hands on the sick, and they shall recover." (Mk.16 v 17-18).

In the book of **Acts in the third chapter and the sixth verse** Peter tells a crippled man who is begging, asking alms, that he has no money to give him, but that he will give him what he has. He then says in the name of Jesus Christ of Nazareth rise up and walk. Peter in affect gave him what Jesus was able to give and would have given him had He still been there. Peter was able to use the name of Jesus just as though it was his own name, and to also operate in the power the name carries on behalf of the man.

He then goes on to declare to all around;

> 12. "........ Ye men of Israel, why marvel ye at this? Or why look so earnestly on us, as though by our own power or holiness we made this man to walk?".....
>
> 16. "And his name (Jesus) through faith in his name hath made this man strong, whom ye see and know: yea, the faith

which is by him hath given him this perfect soundness in the presence of you all."

The Bible tells us that Jesus was the Word of God manifest in the flesh **(Jn. 1 v 14).** Jesus is the name of the Word of God, and there is enough faith in that one name in that one word, to create faith for miracles.

The power and authority in the name of Jesus works the same way today and with the same power as it always did. God has given us this name to use for the benefit of mankind to meet as Jesus did the needs of the people; whether it is in relation to salvation or for healing or any other need such as finances and dealing with demonic powers.

In the first book of **Corinthians the twelfth chapter and the twenty seventh verse** the Bible tells us in black and white in plain speech that we are the Body of Christ; and if the body then the anointed of God, because we've already seen that Christ means the anointed one of God, which is the Word of God and that is Jesus.

So the Bible is telling us that we are the body of Jesus, the body of the Word in the Earth. So you see that we really are Jesus' body on earth and He is our head in Heaven; and the head and body are one therefore God treats us as such. When you say yes but I'm not Jesus, I can't do what He did you are denying what God has said. All it takes is faith in what God has done in relation to us and His Son Jesus the Word, and then we will minister with the same authority over sin sickness and the devil. Hallelujah! Just keep developing in it in faith and it will happen for you.

The Name of Jesus is the most powerful name in the universe when it is used in faith in accordance with the love and will of God the Father. Ephesians tells us to give thanks always for all things unto God in the name of our Lord Jesus Christ. **(Eph. 5 v 20)** Jesus is name above every name and God says we can use that name to live victoriously in this life and faith in that name will secure our life throughout eternity, Thank you Lord. So have faith that when you pray and pray in the Name of Jesus for what you need; that. **<u>God's will to do it for you.</u>** He wants you to have what things soever you ask for in His name.

Chapter Five

If God Be For Us Who Can Be Against Us?
Your Enemy that's Who!

WHEN PAUL MADE the statement in the book of Romans, what he meant after discussing a few things before hand was that ultimately nothing can successfully maintain its opposition against you when God is for you, or on your side, which of course He is when you stand in faith, in confidence that He will deliver you.

> **31. "What shall we then say to these things, If God be for us, who can be against us?"**
>
> **32. "He that spared not his own son, but delivered him up for us all, how shall he not with him also freely give us all things?"**

In the Old Testament good and bad things used to happen and all were attributed to God. These days bad things are still attributed to God by some people usually the unsaved, like storms and earth quakes are called acts of God. This came about because no one actually new they had an adversary, everything that happened was just automatically attributed to God because He was the only person they knew about in the spiritual world. When Jesus the Word of God was manifest in the earth, He began to expose the devil, He taught the disciples how to Deal with him and cast devils out of people and heal infirmities caused by their presence.

People today even in church circles in some cases still find the concept of a devil an evil one that causes bad things to happen, a little hard to swallow. Of course they'd think differently if they had the ability to see what's going on in the spirit realm, but more often than not these people are not in a position to operate in the gifts of the Spirit and see these things.

I was driving home from a service one night and a face appeared in my windscreen. I recognized the man as the husband of a lady that attended our church. While I was looking at the face, another face, one of a demon came out of the man's face and was large in my windscreen. He said to me "We'll see what you believe". I knew instantly what he meant and God put into my mind what I should do and how I should go about it.

On arriving home sure enough there were the man and woman sitting in the lounge room with my wife. I said "hello" and sat down. The woman then proceeded to explain to me that her husband was troubled by a strange occurrence each night as he tried to sleep. I had spoken to this lady before about the erratic behavior of her husband and his seemingly unsociable disposition toward her friends in the church.

It seems that each night he lay down to sleep it was as though he had a giant snake in his belly, and this thing would wriggle and squirm around causing him discomfort and fear. His wife told me she couldn't sleep in the same bed because she could feel this thing moving against her back.

I told the woman that God had shown me the problem and that I knew they would be here when I came home. I explained what I believed to be the problem and at that point realizing his need for Christ and deliverance, the man agreed to pray the prayer of acceptance and submission to Jesus as his Savior. I put my hands on the man's head and I prayed with him as he accepted the Lord.

Then while he was still bowed in prayer I commanded the demon spirit to come out of him and trouble him no more. He said he felt as though it had gone and both were very relieved. It was nice to be able to help it's always a good feeling when God moves and sets someone free of a problem. As nice as it is to be involved and help people they really didn't need me to pray for them, or to cast out that devil. It's just that they didn't know how it could work for them, or that they didn't believe that it would.

When Peter helped the man at the gate (called beautiful) in **(Acts 3 v 6)** and Jesus cast the devil out of the boy in **(Mk. 9 v 25)** and when I prayed for the woman with the Hernia God was working with us. The book of **Acts the tenth chapter** says that;

> **38. "How God anointed Jesus of Nazareth with the holy Ghost and with Power: who went about doing good, and healing all that were oppressed of the devil; for GOD WAS WITH HIM."**

You see that's how you do things you have God working with you; it's not about me or anybody else in particular it's about having faith in God's Word and stepping out. Satan will try and convince you that his authority is greater than yours but it isn't. In **John's first letter chapter four** he is Speaking of powers we will have to contend with and he says this about them and us;

> **"Ye are of God, little children, and have overcome them: because greater is he that is in you, than he that is in the world." (Jn. 4 v 4)**

"Greater is He that is in you" he says, meaning the spirit of God, than he that is in the world, meaning the devils. He goes on to say **in verse five** that;

> **"For whatsoever is born of God overcometh the world: and this is the victory that overcometh the world even our faith." (Jn. 5 v 4)**

Hallelujah God says our faith in Him makes us world over comers. What that means to you and I is that there is nothing in this world that if we put our trust in God we can't overcome. Not sickness, not devils, not poverty, not fear, all things are possible to him that is willing to believe the living Word of God. Jesus said it Himself in the **Gospel of Mark the ninth chapter** when he said;

23. Jesus said unto him, "If thou canst believe, all things are possible to him that believeth." (Mk. 9 v 23)

I know it sounds hard to believe if you haven't heard this before, but believe it you are only limited by your faith in God. No demon in hell can stop you or successfully maintain his presence in your life if you know your authority in God. It might interest you to know also that God is not just a God of big things. He is intimately interested in what you are doing twenty four seven. The other week I had a problem with my knee. I run a lot and that puts a strain on my body from time to time and it seemed as though my knee was about twice the size it should be. Well I went to the doctors to find out what it was that had happened. I believe devils hide behind medical terms. By that I mean we have a situation or symptom caused by evil and we give it a medical name, like epilepsy for example, and from then on we see epilepsy instead of evil, and accept it as something we need medication to cure. He told me it looked as though I would have to go into hospital and have an Arthroscopic clean up. Now Jesus has been my healer for as long as I can remember and I wasn't about to doubt Him now. Even though my leg felt like the doctor knew what he was talking about, I still prefer my own physician, Jesus.

In first Peter chapter two verse twenty four the Bible tells us;

24 "who his own self bare our sins in His own body on the tree, that we, being dead to sins, should live unto righteousness: by whose stripes ye were healed." (1Pet. 2 v 24).

So I received my healing by faith and thanked God for doing it and held my confession of faith for awhile. At first it seemed as though it was getting worse but I've been there many times and I know what I believe and within a week I was running on it again. Praise God no hospital no surgery just the healing power of a loving God. The devil will come to you in these times and try to convince you that it's not working, that you don't deserve to get healed, or he will remind you of something you've done wrong just so you don't feel as though God will do it for you. That's all the power he has over you now. He has to convince you somehow that God didn't mean what He said, when He said,

> "by His stripes ye were (past tense) healed". He did the same thing to Eve in the Garden by saying, "did God really mean you would die?" and to Jesus in the wilderness saying, "if you are the son of God"? etc You see if he can make you doubt he knows you won't get healed and he will be able to stop thanks and praise going to God our Father. Each time you stand for something and he can get you to let go of it by doubting you build one more incident in a track record of failing and that makes it harder for you to be confident the next time.

You see the devil doesn't really care if your saved or not, although he would prefer you go to hell so it grieves God, but what he really hates is a person that is saved and understands their inheritance and the authority that God has given us on the Earth, because those people tear his kingdom down as fast as he tries to build it. There's nothing more dangerous to the devil than a re-born recreated human spirit, filled with the Holy Ghost and Power.

God is good, and the Bible tells us that;

17. "Every good and perfect gift is from above, and cometh down from the Father of lights, with who is no variableness, neither shadow of turning." (Jas.1v17)

It's the devil that is bad, he is our adversary and he is the source of all the evil in the world, Jesus said "you go in my name and police this guy, walk in the dominion that I bought back for you on the cross and live a victorious peaceful productive life to the glory of God" (Robbie paraphrase). **God's will is to do it for you.**

Chapter Six

Faith the Invisible Force? So What is it Exactly?

> **26. "For ye are all the children of God
> By faith in Christ Jesus." (Gal.3v26)**

THE BIBLE TALKS a lot about faith, we discuss faith, we accomplish things we're told by faith and we know from Hebrews the eleventh chapter that God created the worlds with faith;

> **3. "Through faith we understand that the
> worlds were framed by the Word of God, so
> that things which are seen were not made
> of things which do appear." (Heb. 11 v 3)**

So what is it exactly, can we actually describe it, has it got form, or is it something that we are to wonder about until eternities morning when all will be revealed?

In our world there are many different kinds of power. There is Working Power such as a Turbine Engine or Physical Labour and effort, Mind Power, Financial Power etc but there is also the Power of Faith.

The Dictionary describes power amongst other things as;

> "Ability to do or act, a faculty or active property, delegated authority; control, influence, ascendancy......
> Mechanical.....energy applicable to energy or work...
> Force...lly ...having great.

Power, control, influence, energy used to produce, is all terminology that describes something of what faith is. However there is more to faith than these things indicate, although these would be considered correct descriptive words to apply to what we believe faith to be.

Let's look at what the Bible says about faith,

> In the book **of Romans the tenth chapter** we're told that faith comes by hearing, and hearing by the Word of God. In other words our faith increases in an area as we hear God's Word on that particular subject **(Rom. 10 v 17)**.

That incidentally is the only way to get and increase your faith. Many people believe that your faith is increased as it's tested, like lifting weights to build muscle, so you'll hear statements in church such as "how better to increase your faith than to test it"? The problem with that statement is that if it were true every Christian in the world would be a faith giant. There isn't a Christian alive that at some point in their lives, if they've been with God a little while, that hasn't been tested to the limits of their endurance, but are not necessarily any stronger in faith than they were when the trouble started. No it sounds all very religious but when you know your Father properly you'll know he doesn't send the trouble to test you or to build faith in you. The scriptures say;

> 13. "Let no man say when he is tempted, I am tempted of God;"
>
> "For God cannot be tempted with evil, neither tempteth he any man;"
>
> 14. "But every man is tempted, when he is drawn away of his own lusts, and enticed." (Jas. 2 v 13-14)

One of the fist things God told me when I was called to ministry was to "read what was actually in the Word", not to just accept what people preached or told me was in there. He told me to read for myself and when I did I began to see a lot of things that just didn't say what I'd been told. When I started to take notice of what was actually written in the Bible It changed the way I thought about God myself and what God wanted me to have and how to get it. It opened up a whole new world of love and power to me and the ones I loved and ministered to. The Word began to come alive and produce in my life and in the lives of others, just as Jesus said it would.

First of all if your faith is going to work for you as it should, you will have to make God's Word the final authority in your life, because that is what your faith should be based on. The fact that it is what God says it is, and that it works the way He says it will. We'll look at the integrity of the Word or how you can trust God's Word in a later chapter.

What then is Faith? Hebrew's eleven tell us that;

> **"Now faith is the substance of things hoped for, the evidence of things not seen." (Heb. 11 v 1)**

Is Now

The first thing we see about faith is that it is **Now**! If it isn't in the now of your thinking it isn't faith, its hope. Now there isn't anything wrong with hope it's the blessed hope of salvation that fills our hearts with joy when we think of Jesus, God the Father and the Angels. But hope needs to be used in the right place, just as doe's faith, because it's not the same thing. Faith must always be considered in the now, in the present. If it isn't, it means that at that moment you're not considering it to be a done thing, and that in fact your considering it to be something that is coming in the future and frankly tomorrow never comes as they say. No! If it's faith it speaks on this wise;

> **24. "Therefore I say unto you, what things soever ye desire, when you pray, believe that ye receive them, and you shall have them." (Mk. 11 v 24)**

You see the Bible tells us to consider we already have them, and then they will come. In **first Peter the second chapter verse**

twenty four he tells us that by his stripes you were healed. Not will be healed but were healed. You see faith is now, we must consider it done for it to manifest. That's what faith is, the confidence that a thing has been done. So you can see that faith is a now proposition not a future hope.

It's not always easy at first to get hold of this concept. A person might say "well I have believed for my healing", or "I believe God has healed me", and then say "but I wouldn't want to lie about it", so they tell you that they "still hurt" or "it hasn't gone yet". They can't see that by saying "God will heal me" or that "the ailment is still there", that they are putting their healing off to another time doubting God's Word that said you "are" or "were" healed, meaning it is a done thing, and that's what He wants you to confess. after all that's how you got saved remember? Believing in your heart and saying with your mouth for the whole universe to hear. It's the same thing with your healing God wants you to receive it confess it in the now and then He can manifest it on the basis of your faith in His promise.

To have faith is to believe your prayers are answered so faith always says that it's mine, I have it now. Faith never lets go it endures until what we prayed for happens. The Word believes literally means, to act as though a thing was so or already done.

Next we see from the scripture that; **"Now faith is the substance……"** You see faith is isn't anything it is something. It's what the Bible tells us that God made the worlds out of. Too often people act or speak as though faith was just a hairy fairy concept with no real foundation or substance at all. More like an Idea to hold to when all reasonable process has been eliminated. Well faith is a real substance and God used it. What it is not, is a product of human reasoning. In Marks gospel we see that the Chief priests, Scribes and Elders came to Jesus and asked Him who gave Him the authority to do the things he was doing? He said He would answer them if they would first answer Him a question. After some deliberation they chose not to answer Jesus at all, for fear of getting the answer wrong. So He declined to answer there's.

One of the things that God is showing us here is that when it comes to spiritual things man's reasoning without God is useless and will only create fear and the scriptures say that they were afraid to answer Him **(Mk. 11v27-33).**

Faith for healing, to the unregenerated mind is a really silly thing to do. The carnal mind tells us to get to the Doctors and take the medicine or other treatment he gives you. Now don't get me wrong I'm not saying that we shouldn't go to Doctors or take medications. What I am saying is that when your mind is renewed to the possibilities the Word of God offers in regard to healing, and your heart is full of faith, there is a better way than medical science.

You see the first thing the carnal mind thinks of about a situation when human reason without God is concerned is, what happens if this doesn't work? The reason we think this is because in the natural world our senses are what we rely upon to keep us safe. They are what God has given us to operate in or to touch this physical world. Our five senses sight, hearing, smell, taste and touch are how we know what's going on around us, and from that information we know how to react or what needs doing.

The spirit world however is a different proposition those senses won't work out there. That's why we need to rely on the Word of God to teach us how to proceed and what to expect and then trust your Heavenly Father that He knows what He is talking about. After all he made the universe it stands to reason that he would steer you in the right direction with the operation of faith.

Second Corinthians tells us;

> **18. "While we look not at the things which are seen, but at the things which Are not seen: for the things which are seen are temporal; but the things which are not seen are eternal." (11 Cor. 4 v 18)**

There are things in this world that are seen and tangible that we touch with our senses, and there are things which we can't see that God tells us are just as real in the spirit world. These things however must be contacted and dealt with in the realm of our faith life. These things God talks about such as Angels and Heaven etc. were made using the substance of faith.

Some years ago I received a knock at my door, and on answering I was greeted by a man and a woman who were in obvious distress. It turned out that as the woman was pregnant, and had just been for her usual check up. She was about eight months pregnant with a little girl and had just received the news from her doctor that there was no fluid in her womb, and that he thought the baby would be born dead, (still born). They were both very distressed and asked me what they could do, and in fact what could be done at all to help them in this situation? It's at this point when something like this occurs that you find out what you yourself really believe. Do I tell them what the Word says or do I back off in case it doesn't work? And make no mistake the devil will be in your ear.

They had come to me because they knew of my gift from God in the two daughters that I had received against all the odds; and because they had been attending the fellowship where I taught. I opened my Bible and read from the scriptures promising good things, and told them that they could receive their desires if they would only believe. I asked them if they believed the things I had read to them and they indicated that they did. I prayed and asked God to correct this problem and spoke words of life over the unborn child in the Name of Jesus. I prayed for them that their faith not fail and told them to go back and see their doctor the next day, and that things would be ok.

Each time I thought of the couple and their predicament I thanked God for the answer to prayer and for the health of the little one not yet delivered. You see I had to hold my confession of faith because the devil would come to me time and again saying "who do you think you are"? "That's never going to work. These are doctors they know these things". He threw all sorts of stuff at me to try and get me to relinquish my faith in the promises of God. Sometimes it's not easy to stand especially if you're on unfamiliar ground, but we need to do as the Bible tells us and;

> **23. "Let us hold fast the profession of our faith without wavering; (for he is faithful that promised." (Heb. 10 v 23)**

That's what faith is for, to create and to change, when things are going wrong, when things are hard and tough, when your head has no answers. That's when you let your spirit man take over, and listen and believe God's Word over whatever the circumstances say.

The following evening I received another knock at my door, again it was the couple from the previous night. This time they were looking decidedly different. They had big smiles and were excited about their good news. They told me how they had been to their doctors again and had asked him to examine her again. She said the doctor was reluctant to do it, because I guess he was expecting that he would find the same result, and probably thought that the couple was simply having difficulty in accepting the obvious outcome.

On closer examination he realized that her womb was now filled with the fluid that had previously been missing. Overnight God had performed a miracle for the couple. The doctor of course having to be cautious and careful not to give false hope said he was pleased and shocked that her womb was filled with fluid, but strongly suggested that the baby if born alive, would be seriously defected. The couple asked me to pray again but I just encouraged them to hold fast and that it was not necessary. God was working. We were confident that God as it says in Romans chapter four that;

21. "And (Abraham) being fully persuaded that, what he (God) had Promised, he was able to perform." (Rom. 4 v 21)

In the following weeks she gave birth to a healthy little girl, and much praise to her heavenly Father, who had not let her down and had performed that which He had promised. The substance of faith had produced fluid and everything else that was needed to produce the little child that God had intended to live.

A Force

Faith is also **a force,** a creative force, Jesus said in the gospels that it would move a mountain if it was released correctly and not doubted. It would take an enormous amount of force to sling the Universe into existence, and there is a power or force as we've read already that holds it all in place. This is the force of faith.

The most powerful force we have on earth is the Atomic power released through nuclear fission. This power could literally destroy the whole earth if it were used destructively, however the force of faith can not only create blessing in your life but can and did create everything in the known and unknown Universe; and I know this because God said it did, in the book of Hebrews.

Faith power if you like starts where physical powers leave off. When we run out of ways to save ourselves, whether it be for our salvation spiritually, or to mend a broken life, or a broken sickly body, faith power will take over and give us the victory just as it did for the baby in the womb.

I was praying one day in my room just walking slowly up and down talking to God when I thought of a man I knew was in terrible trouble with his health. I said to God "I wish I could go and pray for him and have him get well". You see I had not long received my calling and these things were relatively new to me. I'd heard about healing of course and like many others thought it possible for evangelists and such, but for me to pray and have these things happen was a new concept and quite a challenge to my thinking. Well the Spirit of God spoke to me and said "well go and pray for him then". I was a bit startled and said "is that you God or is it just me thinking it"? Well He didn't say anything else, so in obedience I drove to the house where the man was staying and went inside.

When I had knocked his mother had actually let me in, he had apparently been staying with her because of his illness so she could care for him. The man I had come to see was sitting in an arm chair watching television. I asked how he was feeling and he told me that in the morning he had to go into hospital, and sometime later that day he would have an operation to remove his Pancreas, a piece of his liver, and that they, (the doctors), were concerned about shadows on his lungs.

I asked if he would allow me to pray for him as it was for that reason I believe that God had me come and call on him. He said "ok" but he seemed skeptical, and a little reluctant, and when I said "I'm going to turn the Television down" he was quite annoyed at this. I turned the T.V. down and asked his mother also a believer to lay her hands on him with me and agree that he would receive his healing.

I began to pray and spoke healing into his body commanding the flesh to be whole in the name of Jesus. When I had finished the

Lord spoke to my spirit and told me to tell him that when he went to the hospital tomorrow and had his final ex-ray, or scans before the operation, the Doctor would say to him that, "you have had a miracle and I can't find anything wrong with you in your organs, and your lungs are clear".

Well at this point he turned to me and said "you sound like a gone off Billy Graham and if you've finished could you turn the T.V. back up". I took the Billy comment as a compliment but still felt a little self conscious about the whole business. I tried hard not to think he was ungrateful, remembering from whence I came. I went off to a Bible study meeting and left him with it.

During the study the devil came to me saying "you're going to look stupid when that prayer doesn't work. He'll laugh at you when you see him next he may even be angry for promising him something he didn't get". When this happened and every time I thought of it just as with other things I have prayed for I just thanked God for the result. I wouldn't let go of my faith and so the force of it continued to create. You see the Bible says you can have what you say,

> **Mk 11 v 23**, so satan wants to get you to say that it's not working. He can't stop your prayers Jesus took his authority, which originally was Adam's and gave it back to the born-again man, he can only get you, to stop them coming to pass by getting you, to change what you said.

Anyway a couple of days later I went to the home of this man to enquire of the mother how he was getting along. He apparently, along with his other problems had not been able to eat any proper food for weeks because of ulcers in his stomach. All of his ailments were a result of excessive drinking and smoking over a lot of years.

On arriving at the house I was greeted by this fellow at the door who told me that about two and a half hours after I had prayed he was sitting in the same armchair watching the T.V. when he was catapulted out into the middle of the lounge room floor. As he got up he realized that the sickness in his stomach had gone and as he was hungry and felt as though he would be able to eat. At this point his mother said he began to eat her out of house and home. At the Hospital the next day he had been taken in to have his final scans and ex –rays, after which the doctors told him they could find nothing wrong. He told me the doctor turned to him and said, you have had a miracle. He told everybody he knew for a few weeks, but eventually after some time began to deny the fact of the miracle at all.

You see faith comes by hearing and hearing by the Word of God. Miracles are God's calling card, they show the world that Jesus is alive, but they do not build faith. People say if I could just see I would believe. Jesus said you must believe and then you'll see.

> **40. Jesus saith unto her, "Said I not unto thee, that, if thou wouldst believe, thou shouldest see the glory of God?" (Jn. 11v40)**

Nowhere in the Bible does it say he who sees and believes gets whatsoever he wants. No we must see it through the eye of faith and then we can receive. Jesus rebuked Thomas for needing to see the nail holes in His hands to believe.

Thomas like a lot of people loved Jesus but couldn't bring himself to believe even though Jesus told him before he died that he would rise again. When it came to the crunch, he just couldn't take his word or anybody else's word for it without seeing. He was mentally assenting to the fact that he believed Jesus' words spoken before He left them. He wanted to believe but as we've seen here Jesus was not impressed with his behavior and rebuked him.

> **27. Then Jesus saith to Thomas, "Reach hither thy finger, and behold my hands; and reach hither thy hand, and thrust it into my side: and be not faithless, but believing." (Jn. 20v27)**

Jesus not only rebuked him but said that if you have to see before you believe you are faithless. You have no faith. What we need is to able to believe, not to be faithless, so anything we can discover about faith and its operation will help us in that endeavor, for as we read and learn so faith rises in our heart, because faith comes from the Word. It's like water and wet. You can't have water without wet, so you can't take the Word into your heart without faith growing in relation to the subject your reading.

A Law

The Bible tells us that **faith is also a law**. If something is a law it will work the same way every time in every situation for everybody. That goes for spiritual law or physical laws such as gravity. If you were to throw a ball up in the air it would fall to the ground because of the gravitational pull of the Earth. Now if you gave the same ball to another person and went to a different place and threw the ball a little higher, the ball would still fall to Earth the same way, because gravity is a physical law of the universe.

It's a universal law given by God which will operate the same way every time for anybody, anywhere they invoke it or put it to the test in their lives. God has ordained it in His Word. He said if you believe and say, not doubting you will have what you say, the thing about a law such as faith is that it works for whatever you believe, and is where a lot of God's people come unstuck. They don't realize that it works in both directions. It works good and bad. Am I saying that faith is a bad thing? No I'm not, but it is a consistently the same thing, and that's where people get caught.

You see faith is a consistently the same thing and is no respecter of persons, and doesn't discriminate or make a judgment for itself, so if someone says I am prosperous in the name of Jesus and holds to it God will prosper them. I don't know how, I don't need to that's His job. Ours is just to believe Him. If someone on the other hand though, continually says; that saying stuff doesn't work you'll see them receive nothing and think that they've just proven it to you. The thing about faith is that being a law it will work, but being impartial it will work in both directions, if you are fulfilling the requirement which is to believe and say.

A lot of Christian people will try it for a while and then decide that it doesn't work, but that's because they have little or no faith in operation their just seeing if it works or not. Actually what ends up happening is they fall into the same trap that Thomas fell into in wanting to "see" so they can believe. After a while little or nothing happens for them and they give it away, and some even begin to preach against the faith message, particularly if their disappointment came while believing for someone that was dying or very sick. They are usually hurting and want to find a reason other than a lack of faith to blame. You wouldn't expect to take a new car out without putting fuel in it and then say that it doesn't work. No there are things you need to know, and one of those things is to fuel it up first. A faith life is the same.

We all know a Jumbo Jet can fly. It would have flown a thousand years ago if someone knew how to make it happen. If you took the same Jumbo Jet and stuck It on an Aircraft Carrier and tried to take off, what do you think would happen? Exactly, you'd be swimming in a very short time; because the run way's not long enough. In the same way, although faith is a law and will work, we have to operate in it the way God tells us to. He makes the rules. You need to fill your heart with the Word and then stand when you are convinced of the result.

Faith is your spiritual fuel for miracles, you need to fill your tanks and don't take off until your runway is long enough. Or in other words until you've meditated the Word long enough that it is more real to you than what your standing for or against. Gravity works it's a law, if you throw something up it comes down. Faith works it's a law, if you put the Word in your heart and confess it done and don't relent it will produce every time.

Let's have a look at an example from God's Word of faith working in the negative.

In the Book of Job we read;

> **25. "For the thing which I greatly feared is come upon me, and that which I was afraid of has come unto me." (Job. 3 v 25)**

You see fear is the opposite of faith, there's an old saying fear knocked at the door and faith answered and there was no one there. You can't have fear and faith at the same time. The devil is a fear motivated fear activated being. He is the opposite of God. God is a faith activated faith motivated being. Fear moves satin faith moves God.

What Job was doing, was making sacrifices for his sons, but somewhere along the line he began to lose confidence that they would be ok, so he made more sacrifices, pretty soon he was out of faith and into the thing he feared. He was now in fear not in faith, he was in the devil's hand and his life for a while certainly reflected that state. Eventually he got back into faith, repented and all was well.

The devil had challenged God to stop protecting him and see if he was still loyal to his God. God said to the devil, see, he is in thy power. People preach that God gave Job over to the devil to tempt, but God said see he is in thy hand, in other words I'm not giving him to you he's already there, he put himself there by operating in fear. You see faith will work in the negative if you believe for it. So always make sure your believing and your words reflect what God says in His Word and just as He told Joshua in **(Josh, I v 8 -9)** you'll be successful.

The Apostle Paul writes;

> **27. "Where is boasting then? It is excluded, by what law of works? Nay: but by the law of faith."**
>
> **28. "Therefore we conclude that a man is justified by faith without the deeds of the law." (Rom. 3v 27-28)**

He goes on to say in chapter five that;

> **1. "Therefore being justified by faith, we have peace with God through our Lord Jesus Christ:"**
>
> **2. "By whom also we have access by faith into this grace wherein we stand, and rejoice in hope of the glory of God." (Rom. 5v1-2)**

God has ordained that faith is also a law that by which we can be justified and enter in to the blessed grace where in we are saved. He made it a law so that no principality or power could cause it to be changed and by so doing rob us of the inheritance that God says is ours in Christ Jesus.

A Rest

Wait there's still more good news to do with faith. The Bible tells us in Hebrews that it **is a rest** to the people of God. You see God is a loving God and he loves his children just as we do, and as such doesn't want His kids to have to work any harder than needs be, to get their needs met. He says,

> **9. "There remaineth therefore a rest to the people of God."**
>
> **10. "For he that is entered into his rest, he also hath ceased from his own works just as God did from his."**
>
> **11. "Let us labour therefore to enter into that rest, lest any fall after the same example of unbelief." (Heb. 4v9-11)**

God has ordained that through the sacrificial blood of Jesus there is no longer any need to labour under the curse, or under the restrictions of the law.

What this means to you and I in short is, that we don't have to sacrifice to be forgiven and we don't have to scrape out a living under the curse as Adam did fighting against insurmountable obstacles in life, as so many do.

God is saying here that there is a rest for us, and that rest is the rest that comes from operating in faith. Am I saying that we don't have to work? No but I am saying what the scripture says, in that God gives us the power to get wealth, and ads no sorrow with it (**Prov. 10 v 22**). If we will stay in the Word and in fellowship with the Father, He will show us as He did Joshua, how to be successful and live in peace, and in the prosperity of God, without hating what we do for a living.

There have been times I've spoken to none believers, and listened to their stories of sickness and injury, and I feel sorry for them, if they would only believe, their lives could be so much more like they wished. Unfortunately they just keep saying what they have instead of what they want. No wonder Jesus described people who didn't know the truth as poor in spirit. These folk are just a sad and sorry state going somewhere to happen. I can't imagine going through life without the healing power of God available to me and mine. What a frightening prospect.

There was a time, when my son was young, that he began to get reoccurring ear trouble, lots of ear aches, and this made it difficult for him to sleep, so we would pray and things would be ok for another day, but they would always return. We took him to the doctor and he said that the problem was a common one, and that he would have to have drainage tubes put in. A small operation I was told and nothing to worry about. Well I had even less to worry about because God is my healer and of my family. The next time the devil showed up with his ear ache doctrine, I prayed and rebuked the problem the doctor told me my son had. I spoke healing into his ears commanding them to get in line with God's word, and he never again had the ear aches. That in my book is a better rest from worry than the doctors were offering. You see God's Word is law in the universe and he said if you have faith and pray you will receive. You just have to have faith in your faith, but that's another teaching.

I had a neighbor once that brought his son over because he had unsightly warts on his hands, and they were making him very self-conscious. He brought him to me and asked me to pray for them to go. Again this was very early in my ministry life and I was surprised. I remembered hearing a tape by Kenneth E Hagin where he said he had cursed warts on someone and they left. I thought if it works for him, it will probably work for me, so I said to the warts on his hands, yes I spoke to the warts just as Jesus said speak to the mountain, and told them that "I curse them and send them back to hell where they belong". The boy went home and within a few days the warts had gone completely. What a wonderful loving Father we have. Nothing is too much trouble or too difficult or too small for Him to be interested in if it concerns His children.

Something that faith is not is a feeling. You see because faith is a law, it works as we've discovered the same way all the time. The difference between faith and feeling is that feelings change. Feelings depend on things like physical comfort, and if we are not comfortable with something, or if it hurts, or is embarrassing, we tend to give up on it or shy away from it. That's one of the ways that satan can get us to let go of our healing for instance. He keeps up the pressure and because of the discomfort we think it's not working or it just gets too uncomfortable and we say, "Oh! What the heck, I'll go to the doctor, and stand if something ever comes that they can't cure".

The trouble with that is if you can't get healed of a small thing, a bigger thing God forbid should come, would certainly flatten you. A preacher named Charles Capps said "you start off with the flies and work up to the elephants".

One of my daughters was diagnosed with asthma before I was called to ministry and for three years we were constantly woken up at night with her choking. It was a terrifying experience and we would sleep lightly just waiting for the sound of that coughing and the gasping to breath.

After a while you are so conditioned to waking at the sound that it's like an alarm clock, you wake as it clicks just before it rings. So too with our daughter we would wake just as she started to cough. We would rush her into the bath room and turn on the hot water, allowing the room to fill with steam which would help her breath while at the same time we would be trying to keep her calm, so as she didn't panic. I can't tell you how frightened I was. If it had been blood I would have been ok, I could deal with it, but choking, I was terrified.

So when God spoke to me and said "will you trust me with your children"? I knew what He meant. One afternoon I said to my wife that "faith either works or it doesn't and I believe it does". I took all the medicines that my daughter was taking and threw them out into the garbage I laid my hands on her and prayed.

I rebuked asthma as a name that is named and commanded it to be gone from her in the name of Jesus. I thought my wife believed the same as I did, but when I threw that medicine out, she almost had a fit. I could see the terror in her eyes, and I felt sorry she was scared. I told her to trust me everything would be ok. I believed the Word and I said God has healed her. That night when the coughing started I didn't go into my daughter's bedroom, I stayed in my bed as if nothing was wrong, and I said out loud, "no I don't receive this she is healed, and if she's healed, I won't be getting up".

As it turned out the attack wasn't as bad that night as usual, although it is still hard to hold your nerve in the face of the devil sometimes. That was the last night we ever had any trouble with asthma, and my wife and daughter both were grateful for my faith, and the Goodness of God toward us.

When God said trust me with your children I knew what He meant. I was already trusting God for my own healing but my wife liked to take the children to the Doctor for almost anything and everything. That was only her way of making sure that they were fine so she could rest easy.

There is a better rest though. There remaineth though a rest to the people of God hallelujah, even our faith, and that's a real rest. A real peace of mind because not only do you have peace about what is going on now, but you can rest in your mind about anything that's likely to come up in the future, and that's real peace of mind. Whatever comes our way we have the Word of the living God to rely on, settled in heaven for ever. Labouring to enter into that rest is the kind of work that has no sorrow with it. No sacrificing, just reading God's Word and building faith muscle.

A little earlier I said that the statement how better to increase our faith but to test it, was just religious rubbish, and has no foundation in truth. Well there is another popular belief and that is that if we pray long enough, hard enough, clever enough, or with enough people, or possibly loud enough, our prayers will work. Well they might, God is gracious and if there's anything in there he can move on He will. He's always looking for a way to bless us. The sad fact is though that prayer doesn't make faith work, faith makes prayer work. I'm going to say that again, faith makes prayer work, prayer doesn't make faith work. If you haven't got any faith working you can pray till the cows come home to no avail. God is not moved by your circumstance, remember, we looked at that earlier, faith moves God, not troubles.

The reason he's ordained it that way is because that keeps the devil out of our and God's business. You see he doesn't have any faith he operates on fear, but he'll try to con you, and he will, if you let him, he's had plenty of time to smooth out his act. So don't fall into the trap of thinking that just because you've got others with you that they may take up the slack. Let me show you something from the Word about this;

Now in the book of Acts, Peter got himself thrown into jail for preaching and teaching about Jesus. In chapter twelve verse five it says that prayers were made without ceasing of the church unto God for him. Ok we've got a whole bunch of people praying flat out, twenty four seven for Peter's safety, and no doubt his release. People had a tendency to not last long in Herod's prisons.

In the following verses, the Bible tells us how an Angel came and woke Peter and they left the prison. It's all good news so far, until Peter gets to the door of the place at which this crowd was praying for him.

> **13. "And as Peter knocked at the door of the gate, a damsel came to hearken, named Rhoda."**
>
> **14. "And when she knew Peter's voice, she opened not the gate for gladness, but ran in, and told how peter stood before the gate."**
>
> **15. "And they said unto her, Thou art mad. But she constantly affirmed that it was even so. Then said they, it is his Angel."**
>
> **16. "but Peter continued knocking: and when they had opened the door, and saw him, they were astonished." (Acts. 12 v 13-16)**

Now we can see from this passage what I'm saying. All these people were gathered to pray for Peter, supposedly in faith, and I'm sure that Rhoda did, but I'm not too sure about the rest of them, because, had they been exercising faith they would not have been surprised at Peter's arrival at the door. Even if they were surprised he had come so quickly, I doubt that they would have told Rhoda that she was mad for believing he had come from the jail. No I think Peter got out of Jail on her prayers. The Bible says that the effectual fervent prayer of a righteous person avails much. **(Jas. 5 v 16)**

When you ask others to pray with you for someone or for your needs, make sure these people are in agreement with you, in the Word of faith, and don't just have a religious idea about God. The Bible says in Matthew that if two of you agree as touching anything on earth, that God will give it you **(Matt. 18 v 19)**.

When the scripture says agree it's not enough that you agree on what you are asking for. If you are going to pray on the basis of that scripture then you should make sure you agree on what the Word says about it and what God has promised, and then pray the way the Word tells us that we should. If we're going to pray we might as well get what we're asking for.

Something else to watch out for when you make your stand and decide to live the faith life is people. When one of my children was small about the time they began to read, one of their eyes began to turn in each time they would try to focus on the words. It was a sickening thing to watch and caused them great difficulty when trying to read their little school reader. Why the problem showed up when it did and not before I don't know, but I did know I wasn't going to let it stay.

The day this child of mine was born and came into the world I was like most parents, exited at the arrival of this little person that had never been around before, there had been some problems along the way but finally the day had arrived and here they were. The doctor came out to see me and said these words to me: "congratulations you have a perfect baby boy". Well I was over joyed and very relieved because as I said there had been a few hiccups.

I told him that I was going to pray for him about his eye, and that God was going to heal him. Now some might say that telling him that God was going to heal him was a mistake, what if it didn't work, what if God didn't heal him? He would be very disappointed; well we both would but that couldn't be true because you see God has already healed us on the cross at Calvary. The Bible tells us that He took the stripes that bought our healing for us. He took our sickness, our diseases, our mental pressure and our sin, then went to hell and became poor and a social outcast, so as to substitute for us in every area. We don't need to be sick because Jesus was already sick for us. satan is the author of sickness disease and abnormalities and Jesus stripped him of his right to put that stuff on us anymore. Our part in it all is to just receive healing and correction of ills by faith. That's all He asks us to do, hold fast our profession of faith **(Heb 10 v 23)**. The other reasons I told him God would heal him was firstly so his confidence in the fact that his Heavenly Father wanted him to be well and that He wanted to do it for him would Increase, also I wanted to put myself in a position where if God didn't move I would be in trouble. You see by putting God on the spot so to speak puts the pressure on the devil. I put myself in a position where God has to move or he lets me down. I know He likes that because it shows Him that I have enough faith to put myself in that position. God loves you to act on your faith; the Bible teaches that it pleases God.

The Word says in Matthew, as we've already seen, that two can agree on something and it will be done for them By God, so I went to a friend of mine who I knew was a man of faith and I told him I was going to pray for my son and I wanted him to agree with me about his healing.

I prayed for my son but we saw no immediate improvement I was confident in God though that it was a done thing. My boy went to school day after day with no sign of improvement. He was going to a Christian school at the time so I explained that we had prayed and that we believed God had healed him. For awhile they seemed to accept the fact but slowly as days became weeks and then more weeks they began to put pressure on me to have him operated on. This was the norm apparently to fix this condition; of what I was later told was a lazy eye problem. This is a condition where a muscle on one side of the eye is too weak to do its job properly and straighten the eye forward for focusing on a book page for instance. The remedy for this was to fix the muscle in the correct position to look forward and read, but this also meant that he would not be able to move the eye in time or in line with the other and so would always appear as a defective eye.

Now these people meant well and I'm sure, they genuinely believed that I was off the track with this kind of thinking, they called it hyper faith. This is a term given to a faith that has no real basis or foundation on which to make such claims or have any such expectation of such. As I said these people were sincere but I believed sincerely wrong. As the weeks dragged on it was hard to look at my son struggle but I was determined not to have him go through life with an eye in a fixed position. I told you that you need to watch out for people, you see if someone hasn't got the revelation of healing that you have they start saying things like, well it's obviously not working or I think it's about time you let the Doctors fix him up and eventually these comments progress to harsher words like we think, (now there ganging up), it's we think that you may be a little spiritually proud and off on a bit of a tangent. Finally I was getting comments relating to not caring about my son and verging on false doctrines and heresies, because people become afraid when they don't understand.

I told them that we were standing in faith that God had healed my son and that if they would agree with me on this thing it would probably happen a lot quicker. Now that may have been a little blunt or even a little bit rude but I was starting to feel annoyed that they were letting the devil use them to attack my faith in the finished work of the Cross.

The scripture I was standing on was in James where it is written;

**17. "Every good gift and every perfect gift
is from above, and cometh down from the
Father of lights, with whom is no variableness,
neither shadow of turning." (Jas. 1 v 17)**

Remember I told you that when my son was born the Doctor told me that God had given me a perfect child, and as such I was not going to let the devil make him imperfect. Every time I saw my son's eye turn, every single time, I said no I don't receive that, that eye is well.

It took some time and a lot pressure from a lot of people who thought they were doing God's work in opposing me, just as Paul thought he was when he was Saul and he persecuted the church. Eventually I was watching him read one day and his eye didn't turn and never ever turned in again. God is faithful that promised and is always true to His word. Why it took seven months to get our healing that time I don't know. Why it took two and a half hours for the man to be healed in his armchair I don't know, why the woman with the bleeding hernia was healed on the spot and then was healed of arthritis the following morning as she thanked God at breakfast I don't know. I don't have to know, because that's God's business, and if He chooses to tell me I'll operate with that extra knowledge as well. All I have to know is that faith works it's a law that works every time and it's a rest to the children of God. I know also that it is a force that no devil in hell can resist and it is a now for now proposition and I thank God for it. Another reason it works so well is this;

**20. "…………: And the life which I
now live in the flesh I live by the faith**

> **of the Son of God, who loved me, and
> gave himself for me." (Gal 2 v 20)**

It's His faith that we live by. The faith is Jesus' faith and His faith will not fail, so have some faith in that fact. Read it over and over until you get a revelation that the faith you are using is God's faith. Where else would it have come from in the first place? He said in scriptures what have you got that you did not receive. God has given us His faith to use to believe;

> **17. "For therein is the righteousness of God
> revealed from faith to faith: as it is written.
> The just shall live by faith." (Rom.1v17)**

You are a faith being just as God is a faith being, you were born of His Word, you are a new faith creature not the old you, and you have the right to live by faith victorious in every part of your life Spiritually, Mentally, Physically, Financially and Socially that's every area of human existence;

> **23. "Being born again, not of corruptible seed,
> but of incorruptible, by the Word of God, which
> liveth and abideth forever." (1Pet. 1 v 23)**

We were born anew by the Word of God when we accepted Jesus as our Lord and Savior.

You may not have thought about it this way, but you are not really related to your Mother and Father the same way you were before. God tells us to honour them, but our Father is now God. A lot of people think about that in terms of just metaphorical but it is a literal fact. God is not in the habit of saying things that are not exactly true, He doesn't say things just because they may sound impressive as man does or just to emphasize something. If He said it it's true and it's done.

He tells us that we are born of the Word. That should help you with your confidence and boldness toward Him, when you think that you are a brand new person made of faith and born of the Word from the very heart of God. How would He ever deny you anything?

17. "Therefore if any man be in Christ, he is a new creature: old things are passed away; behold all things are become new." (11Cor. 5 v 17)

We hear this scripture quoted on Sundays in church and in teaching sessions and we read in our own reading time, but until you stop and think about the enormity of what this is saying, we won't understand the gravity of this statement. We are literally a different person as far as God is concerned and we should be accepting the truth of it as well. Once this happens it becomes a lot easier to believe God would do something you ask, than you did in the past. Remember God wants to do for us it's just that we stagger at the promises being weak in faith. We begin to doubt sometimes because the devil reminds us of our failures and weaknesses. Now however we can think on the scripture and be more confident that our requests will be met.

Next time you are faced with an obstacle that is stopping you from living in victory say to your mountain in the name of Jesus get out of my way I'm a child of God and you've already lost. The devil knows it he just wants to see if you know it. Tell him who you are and command sickness to leave in the Name of Jesus.

The Bible says;

3. "…………according as God has dealt to every man the measure of faith." (Rom. 12v3)

The measure is the same measure that God raised Jesus from the dead with, it's the same measure he used to give you your rebirth, if God hadn't given us the same measure of faith as he gave Jesus, it would be unjust for Him to tell us that we could move mountains or pray and see people recover.

The secret as to why Jesus was more successful was that He knew how to release His faith, He knew how to use His faith, and He had confidence that His faith would work for Him. Jesus would spend time talking to the Father listening to His words. He said "I only do what the Father tells me" He fellowshipped with the Father just as we can. We can fellowship with God by staying in His Word reading what He says.

If you can, imagine your measure of faith is in you, inside your new recreated being, but it's in seed form, so it's like being given a big measuring scoop full of faith when you were made alive unto God, when you got saved. Now this faith as with other seed is only good when it is planted or used correctly.

> 22. "But the fruit of the Spirit is love, joy, peace, longsuffering, gentleness, goodness, FAITH."
>
> 23. "Meekness, temperance: against such there is no law." (Gal. 5 v22-23)

God has planted your faith correctly it's in good ground in your re-born recreated spirit and alive unto God, but like all seed it needs to develop, and the way you develop seed into something useful is to feed and water it.

> 2. "As newborn babes, desire the sincere milk of the Word that ye may grow thereby:" (1Pet. 1 v 2)

Paul speaking of Christ and his love for the church says;

> 26. "That he might sanctify and cleans it by the washing of the water by the Word." (Eph. 5 v 26)

The Bible tells us that we are to desire the Word and that Christ washes and cleanses us with the Word. It's the Word that causes the church to develop into what God wants it to be, and it's the Word that develops feeds and waters the seed of faith that is in us as fruit of the spirit. God is using His faith here speaking those things that are not yet as though they were, by calling your faith seed as already developed fruit. How does He know they will develop? Because He is a faith person and Paul tells us in Philippians that;

> 6. "Being confident of this very thing, that he which has begun a good work in you will perform it until the day of Jesus Christ:" (Phil. 1 v 6)

So you can be confident also that since God has promised to keep working on you, developing you, and growing as it were you toward a crop of fruit, and in this case, a crop of faith fruit for you to use as a servant, to work for you as you work for Him. **God's will is to do it for you**, He wants to.

Chapter Seven

The Honesty and Integrity of God's Word

> **11. "So shall my Word be that goeth forth out of my mouth:**
>
> **It shall not return unto me void, but it shall accomplish that which I please,**
>
> **And it shall prosper in the thing whereto I sent it" (Isa. 55 v 11).**

SO FAR WE'VE looked at the fact that God want to do things for us, that he says He is moved by our faith on our behalf, that we have victory over devils, he's told us what our faith is and what it will do, and the Bible even explained how we are to use our faith and that we have a right to use the name of Jesus as our own.

All this information and these promises are wonderful of course, but they hinge on one very important issue, whether or not the words of the one who makes the promise are trust worthy and reliable. There's a couple of things that come into that, such as; Is the person genuine when he says the words and is that person actually able to deliver what he has promised?

In the above scripture the Lord had said that His word shall be. In other words it will definitely do what it was sent to do. Let's have a look at some of the incidents that put God's Word to the test. The Bible tells us that;

> **1. "In the beginning God created the heavens and the earth." (Gen. 1 v 1)**

Well has anybody seen a heaven and earth around here lately? So I guess that one came to pass.

We've already seen the scripture in Hebrews;

> **3. "Through faith we understand that the worlds were framed by the word of God, so that things which are seen were not made of things which do appear." (Heb. 11 v 3)**

God's desire was to create, so He spoke His word and the worlds came into being. Every word that God speaks instantly becomes so. It may not appear straight away but if it's been spoken it is done. Your salvation in Jesus Christ is assured on the basis of your faith in Him because God decreed it so.

In Genesis when God was speaking with Abram he said to him;

> **4. "As for me behold, my covenant is with thee, and thou shalt be a father of many nations.**
>
> **5. "Neither shall thy name any more be called Abram, but thy name shall be Abraham; for a father of many nations have I made thee." (Gen. 17 v 4-5)**

Notice that in verse four He said "I will make you" and then in verse five He says "I have made you". What happened between **verse four and verse five** to cause him to go from Abram a guy on his own with no family to a guy who was married and a father of a multitude, nations full of children? I'll tell you what happened. God spoke that's what happened. You see when God speaks it becomes universal law for ever for eternity. Such is the integrity and the power of God's word that he created the universe by telling it to be there. That's why God will never say anything negative about you in any way, because if He did it would be with you forever.

Now I said before that it may not appear straight away but it has to happen if God has said it. Abram did become the father of many nations, because God changed his name to Abraham which means father of many nations before he even had one son. Note too that by changing his name to Abraham every time he said his name he was confessing that he was the father of many nations, he was confessing that which God had said and it will work exactly the same way for you when you speak out words of faith in the name of Jesus, because God has said it just as He said Abram was Abraham. We have only to look around the world to see that the word concerning Abraham was fulfilled.

Peter tells us that even though he was witness with his eyes on the holy mount as he calls it. He saw Jesus lighted with the Gory of God, and heard God say "this is my beloved Son", and yet he tells us that we have a more sure word of prophecy, in other words he is saying that you can trust the written word even more than you could trust a voice or seeing angels.

The Amplified Bible puts it this way;

> 19. "And we have the prophetic word (made) firmer still. You will do well to pay close attention to it as to a lamp shining in a dismal (squalid and dark) place, until the day breaks through (the gloom) and the Morning Star rises (comes into being) in your hearts." (11 Pet. 1 v 19) Amp. Bible

Such is the Integrity of the written Word of God that Peter himself tells us it is better than seeing. You see we can be deceived by our eyes, you've only got to drive until you get tired or watch a shell game or watch something produced electronically these days to realize that you can't be sure of what you are seeing. It's not good to base or risk your life on what something looks like either, feelings and appearances are no guarantee of the truth or success, however Peter tells us the Word of God is a more sure word. If Jesus were on the Earth today and was moving about the town, we could ask Him to teach us and to heal us. He isn't doing that now He is in Heaven, on the right hand of the father, as our High Priest interceding for us.

What we do have though is the Word of God and it takes the place of the person of Jesus. People think that the Holy Spirit is replacing Jesus but that's not right. Never has the Holy Spirit been referred to in the scriptures as the Word only Jesus.

The Bible tells us in the Gospel of John;

> 14. "And the Word was made flesh, and dwelt among us, (and we beheld his glory, the glory as of the only begotten of the Father,) full of grace and truth." (Jn. 1v14)

The Word became flesh and dwelt amongst us so that we could see the truth. The people and religious leaders of the time were so far away from what God wanted them to be like, He sent Jesus to show them physically what the Word looked like in action. He was literally the living Word of God. The Bible says that we are now the Body of Christ on the earth, because Jesus is our Head and He is in Heaven, so we are to act as He did on earth and He will be talking and praying as we might be if we were there. Jesus will always have the preeminence of course. That's why so many scriptures refer to us as being in Christ or in Him. Spending time in the Word is spending time with Jesus. He is the Word of God so every word in the bible is Him and He is in each word. Soaking in the Word is soaking in Jesus. So many times I've heard people say I wish Jesus were here, I've said it myself. The Bible tells us in Romans;

> 6. "But the righteousness which is of faith speaks on this wise, Say not in thine heart, who shall ascend to Heaven? That is to bring Christ down from above)."
>
> 7. "Or who shall descend into the deep? (that is, to bring up Christ again from the dead)."
>
> 8. "But what saith it? The word is nigh thee, even in thy mouth, and in thy heart: that is, the word of faith, which we preach."(Rom. 6-8)

Jesus the Word of God is in your mouth and heart. The bible is telling us not to call Jesus up or down, but to speak Him out believing and God will manifest it for you.

He will become the flesh you need, He will become the finances you need and He will become the **"whatsoever things you desire when you pray."**

I don't believe in noisy faith, or manipulating people by slipping into conversations with people, or preaching needs I think they may be able to meet. I tell the Lord and receive the need met and expect it to come about. On one occasion I needed some money and I received a large sum of money under my front door mat. I still don't know who put it there. On another occasion I went into a store and selected a new jacket it was a beautiful blue with silver buttons. The sales assistant asked if I would take it and I said that I was just picking it out, and would get the money from my Father and return. I asked the sales assistant if he wouldn't mind holding it for me. He said he would and casually asked me who my father was. I replied that it was God. At this point the assistant looked at me and said "oh one of those are you"? From the look on his face I could tell that he thought I was a weirdo.

A couple of days later I received a sum of money and a set of car keys in the letter box of my home. I went straight into town and bought my jacket much to the surprise of the assistant. God loves to do things for His kids. The Bible says that God knows our needs before we even ask for them. Sometimes He'll give you things you don't even ask for if you remember to give Him the thanks for everything.

In the Gospel of John chapter seventeen we read where Jesus is praying for the Disciples, He says that not only is He praying for them, but for all that come to believe on their word. That includes all of us indirectly so it's important that we know what He's asked for because then we can believe for it.

15." I pray not that thou shouldest take them out of the world, but that thou shouldest keep them from the evil."

16. "They are not of the world, even as I am not of the world."

> 17. "Sanctify them through thy
> truth: thy Word is truth."
>
> 18. "As thou hast sent me into the world,
> even so have I sent them into the world".
>
> 19. "And for their sakes I sanctify myself,
> that they also might be sanctified
> through the truth." (Jn.17v15-19)

Jesus asked that we be sanctified through the word. The word sanctifies means to set apart for some special reason. One definition says to "sanctify is to make holy, consecrate, to purify from sin". God through the miracle action of his living word has purified us set us apart for Him. Well what are we set apart from, and why did we need to be set apart? Jesus in His prayer asked that we not be taken out of the world but that we might be kept from the evil that is in the world because of sin that is created and perpetually generated by the devil. He desired that although we need to live here, work here, and minister here in His name bringing the good news of the Gospel to all men, we don't need to be a part of all the things that go on here. I'm not just talking about doing obvious evil like stealing or fornicating etc. I believe He set us apart by the sanctifying power of His Word from the evils of sin, sickness, poverty and mental pressures etc. These are all evils as far as God is concerned and not just a natural part of the life that we are all living. Nowhere in the Bible does it say we have to put up with such things or live under such circumstances.

The book of Ephesians tells us;

> 21. "If so be that you have heard him, and have
> been taught by him, as the truth is in Jesus:"
>
> 22. "That you put of the former
> conversation the old man, which is corrupt
> according to the deceitful lusts;"
>
> 23. "And be renewed in the spirit of your mind."

24. "And that you put on the new man, which is created in righteousness and true holiness." (Eph. 4 v 21-24)

We see here that the Word of God also sanctifies us from the old sin nature, from the old self that was separated from God and was dead in sin.

The Apostle Paul tells us in an earlier chapter, that we were once walking according to what he calls the course of this world or in other words, we were carried along in the river of life with no hope of changing ourselves into holy people. We had no way of making ourselves acceptable to God and we were, therefore lost. We were living our lives just as satan wanted us to, and doing the things that were not good for us in terms of reaching our full potential.

Only in God can we ever hope to do the miraculous things that Jesus did when he walked the earth. Our minds, even if we think we were not really bad people, in that we didn't hurt anyone, were still in enmity with God, we were still disqualifying ourselves from real peace of mind and fellowship with God by virtue of the fact that our spirits were dead in our sins; hence our thought life was not acceptable. The Bible tells us that God quickened us or made us alive to Him. (The word quick is in relation to the quick on your finger nail. If you pull your nail too far down the finger it suddenly becomes alive with pain). In the same manner God tells us by the action of the word of God we suddenly became alive, able to sense spiritual things and the love of the Father in us toward others. God knows our every thought Hebrew tells us;

12. "For the word of God is quick, and powerful, and sharper than any two edged sword, dividing asunder of soul and spirit, and of the joints and marrow, and is a discerner of the thoughts and intent of the heart." (Heb. 4 v 12)

The Word of God separates us from the world by causing us to be born unto God by faith. It also separates us from the world by showing up the world to our spiritual senses, what is to be avoided and why and also separates the thoughts of the mind. It's a discerner of the intent of the heart. Yes God sees the real motives behind our actions but it also shows us of our selves. The Word enables us to see ourselves objectively instead of always subjectively. In my counselling sessions I help people to realize what they've been doing, sometimes without realizing, and how they might get to where it is that they think they might like to be. I also examine with them why they feel they need to be in that place. I like philosophy and psychology, I like to unravel the strings of thought and help people understand how to think clearly, and keep things in perspective. I help them stay away from blob thinking as I call it. Like when play-doe's different colours all get mixed to together and they become a brown blob.

So too, thoughts all run together when you find that you are under stress with no coping skills to deal with it all. God's Word tells us that it has the power in it to discern between thoughts and the intent of the heart. It will clear your thinking for you and stop you fooling yourself, if you are honest in your desire to do what it says, and are happy and obedient to receive instruction.

God gave us His Word to clear up our thinking. If we will put the Word first place in our lives, and accept what God says over what we think, we will deal in life with good success. In fact the Bible tells us that the Word will transform our thinking and it says in **(Prov. 23v 7)** that as a man thinketh in his heart so is he. In other words the Word teaches you how to think and because you think that way, you'll act that way, and because you act that way, you'll receive the things in life that change it for the better. Sow a thought reap an action, sow an action reap a life style, sow a life style reap a life.

Everyone's life to a greater extent is a result of their thinking over the years.

Where you and I are today is a direct result of our thinking.

> **2. "And be not conformed to this world: but be ye transformed by the renewing of you mind, that you may prove what is that good, and acceptable, and perfect will of God." (Rom. 12 v 2)**

The world continually tries to influence us in the direction of the world. We are bombarded with advertising in relation to everything we come in contact with in this life; and the main purpose of it, is to firstly let us know what's available, and them to become dissatisfied with what we already have, so that we'll go out and buy what's on offer in the add. The campaign seeks to achieve conformity to the world's way of thinking; for example we need this, we should have that, we deserve her/him etc. The Bible says the Word of God will transform us, change us into what is most productive for us in our Christian life. We will be changed by the Word. It has the power to change us to be more Christ like. We are born male and female but it is Christ likeness that makes us real men and women.

When Jesus walked the earth there was nothing He came up against that defeated him, not sickness, not devils, not the need for money, not even death could hold him. He was a total success in everything He did. Jesus as we've already seen was the Word of God in action in the earth. There was never a situation where the Word was stuck for an answer. When he needed to feed five thousand people He just fed them. You see the Word has the power in itself to bring itself to pass.

> **18. "The Spirit of the Lord is upon me, because he hath anointed me to preach the Gospel to the poor; he hath sent me to heal the broken hearted, to preach deliverance to the captives, and recovery of sight to the blind to set at liberty them that are bruised,"**
>
> **19. "To preach the acceptable year of the Lord." (Lk.4 v18-19)**

The Word of God was sent to accomplish the saving, delivering, releasing, providing, protecting ministry that Jesus' ministry on Earth exemplified, and it is still here today. Jesus left and when He did He sent the Holy Spirit to teach, comfort and guide us, but He didn't take the written Word out of the earth with Him. The Word in all its power is still here to create in our lives. It's to be respected and received in faith trusting that it will perform that which God has sent it to do. "............**but it shall accomplish that which I please, and it shall prosper in the thing where unto I sent** it." **(Isia. 55 v 11)** Well what did He send it to do? Everything that God's Word has promised us that God wants us to have.

We can trust the word because it's the same word as when He made the worlds, the same word that Jesus was, and the same word that has raised you from being dead in sin. God and his Word are one. **<u>It's God's will to do it for you,</u>** and it's His Word that is here to do it for you.

Chapter Eight

Your Inner Image of Yourself. Creates Your Future

A LONG TIME ago the devil told a lie and the world, the Church, and Mankind in general believed it, and still does. The devil told the people of the world that God was mad at them and that He's just looking for an excuse to punish people, and religious minded people who don't know God and that would rather hang on to their church positions, the control and prestige and what little power they feel they have over people, have continued perpetuating such false hoods, instead of finding out what God really thinks.

We are continually told by all sorts of people such as pastors, evangelists, friends and relatives etc. that God will only do things for people if they follow their particular church rules, or one I particularly dislike is the phrase it's ok to believe God but we must be sensible about this, you need a balanced Christian life" and we do. What they mean though is that you shouldn't go out on a limb trusting God, or you'll get over into a hyper faith area and come crashing down into a heap or worse, maybe even die believing God for something you're not going to get. Their idea of a balanced faith life is one with a balance of faith and unbelief. An example of this is where you say you have believed God for your healing, and then you go to the doctors for him to fix you up. There's nothing wrong with going to the Doctors as I've said earlier, but if you have a foot in both camps you're a double minded person and the Bible says you won't receive from the Lord. This is not because He's punishing you but because He can't get in there with you until you're in faith. If you're sitting in the Doctor's office waiting for him to give you something or to do something to correct the problem, as I said there's nothing wrong with going to the Doctors, but you're hardly exercising faith in God's Word that say's "by His stripes you ARE healed" are you? If you're believing that God will help the medication work better or faster than it has in the past, well at least that's a step in the right direction, and that's ok if that's all the faith you have right now, but at least you're taking the first step to a life where God is your absolute healer. A point I feel I need to make here is that throwing your medication away doesn't make your faith work better, or make God move. Throwing away your glasses doesn't make your healing for your eyes work. A woman asked me after prayer should I throw away my glasses. I said if you have to ask then you'd better keep them. Do you see the difference?

> **6. "But let him ask in faith, nothing wavering. For he that wavereth is like a wave of the sea driven with the wind and tossed."**
>
> **7. "For let not that man think that he shall receive any thing of the Lord."**
>
> **8. "A double minded man is unstable in all his ways." (Jas. 1 v 6-8)**

You see God wants us to be sure which way you want to proceed and then he will put his power behind you to create the thing you have believed him for, not believing, but that, you have, past tense, believed Him for.

Then there's the just straight out "who do you think you are"? People, who say, "who are you expecting God to do that for you"? In their hearts they are saying" I couldn't believe for that and I know about the things of God much more than you do". It actually makes some people mad when you tell them what you have believed God for. It makes it hard to have an inner image of yourself being or doing in God, when the people around you are constantly negative in their approach to the Word or your faith stands, particularly if they're always judging your requests of God as spiritually proud and big headed. The old saying birds of a feather flock together is a good thing to remember here. It's better to be around like minded people, those that will believe God with you, and who are happy when you get the victory.

The mindset that the doubting people have, which tells them that God won't move for them, and the reason that others are mad at you, actually comes from a sin consciousness. Now if you were to say to them that they have a sin consciousness they would say "that's rubbish" and how dare you accuse them of such a thing? They actually think they are being humble toward God but it's a false humility. A humble person would take God's word that they are worthy to receive, just because He said so.

That's how the devil gets them to think that God won't do the things they want because they're not worthy of the asking. If they do ask and they don't get it, instead of realizing their faith isn't developed enough in that area, they would rather just say, "I guess God just didn't want us to have it". It comes from a lack of righteousness consciousness. The mindset that says God is sovereign and if he wants me to have that He would give it to me, I don't have it, so I don't deserve it, or He would have given it to me. Yes God is sovereign but He has told us to ask what you will. The person that moves on the Word of God and receives is the person that says, "God is my loving Father so why if He has said I can have whatsoever, why wouldn't I be able to get it. Thank you for it Father". This person has a better developed inner image of themselves than the other person. The inner image that says, "God has made me righteous so I do deserve it". This is the man that puts faith in the finished work of the cross.

In the book of John we read;

> **12. "Then spoke Jesus again unto them saying, I am the light of the world: he that followeth me shall not walk in darkness, but shall have the light of life." (Jn. 8 v 12)**

The Bible tells us that Jesus is the light of the world, and light helps us see an inner image of ourselves that may not be visible without the light of the power of God's Word in our thinking. We need to have the light turned on inside of us, in our thinking to the possibilities of what we could achieve if there wasn't anything we couldn't do.

This light that can shine on the inside is wisdom, truth, possibilities, ideas and witty inventions the Bible says in **Proverbs eight verse twelve**. You've heard the saying I'm sure that when someone got an idea that hey the light came on. Jesus is the light of the world. The Word is the light to the world in a dark and dangerous place and time.

Modern sports psychologists these days have discovered something the Bible has been telling us for centuries, that if you form a mental image of yourself doing something and rehearse it over and over in your mind, when it comes time to perform it, you have a much better chance of actually achieving what you desired. They have discovered that the brain can actually learn to do something without actually physically practicing it. Well isn't that a new thing? Well no, not really does this sound familiar;

7. "For as a man thinketh in his heart, so is he." (Prov. 23 v 7)

We think we're so clever don't we mankind? A survey team asked students in an American college, if God was real, do they think that He understands radar? The majority answered no. Who do they think gave the bat his radar, or the Dolphin its sonar, or a fish the ability to navigate its way back to the exact same stream to spawn, that it left from to travel the oceans of the world for five years? Well God did of course.

God teaches in the Bible to ask for what we want, but that doesn't always have to be things. I was talking to a youth group at a meeting on a Friday night and I said "if you could ask for anything you wanted of God what would you ask for?" Well I got lots of answers like a new car, a trip, money, that sort of thing. I said to the group what about being able to operate in the gifts of the Holy Spirit, asking God to allow you to become proficient in Prophecy or blessed with special powers to heal? You see we limit God's work in us, by limiting our own vision of ourselves.

14. "Ye are the light of the world. A city that is set on a hill cannot be hid (Matt 5 v 14).

Jesus tells us here that we are the light of the world just as He said He was. We are the word on the earth remember? He says we should shine as though we were a brightly lit city on a hill, where people from miles around could see its light shining so bright it was impossible to hide it. The world should see us shining in the glory of the power of our God, demonstrating to the world that Jesus is alive by our miraculous lives. There is no earthly reason, no heavenly reason, and no reason in hell why we can't dream a dream that takes our breath away, and see God bring it to pass, when it involves winning this world to Jesus. The Bible tells us that God gives us the desires of our heart;

> **4. "Delight thyself also in the Lord; and he shall give thee the desires of thine heart."**
>
> **5. "Commit thy way unto the Lord; trust also in him; and he shall bring it to pass." (Psalm. 37 v 4-5)**

Hallelujah what a fantastic promise. God says He will give you the desires of your heart. So first of all God puts a desire in your heart he knows will stimulate, satisfy, excite, comfort and challenge you, and then He allows you the privilege of asking for it. He then says yes to your request, and then manifests it in your life as you stand in faith, because He wants you to be happy and enjoys being a co labourer with us. It just doesn't get any better than that. It's a family business. God is healing our nation and He's using His Spirit filled, faith talking, word believing, re-born people to build the Kingdom. The inner image of God created the universe, and the inner image in us will create our future.

> **1. "Be ye therefore followers of God, as dear children." (Eph 5 v 1)**

We are to be followers of God, that means we are to follow His actions, to be imitators of God, do things the way he does them, follow His example of faith in action, visualize the picture of what you want to create, and then speak your words of faith, stand your ground and watch it happen.

Up until I was about thirty three years old, as a result of my upbringing and lack of support from my parents, I had not developed any real self esteem. I was not shy, I had a temper, but I was afraid to speak up or step forward to do something even if inside I knew I could do it. I just simply lacked the confidence to have a go. I had developed a way of thinking which basically, blamed everyone else for me not getting ahead. I thought everyone was against me, rather than realizing it was the way I was reacting to things that happened in my life that was making it difficult for me to get ahead.

Then came the day the Lord called me to ministry. I was sitting at my kitchen table reading Timothy when the words I was reading suddenly became bigger, clearer and more defined on the page. They were the words in the verses;

> 2. "Preach the word; be instant in season, out of season; reprove, rebuke, exhort with all longsuffering and doctrine."

> 3. "For the time will come when they will not endure sound doctrine; but after their own lusts shall they heap to themselves teachers, having itching ears;"

> 4. "And they shall turn away their ears from the truth, and shall be turned unto fables,"

> 5. "But thou in all things, endure afflictions, do the work of an evangelist, make full proof of thy ministry." (11Tim. 4 v 2-5)

I was startled, for one thing I was not exactly a model Christian by any stretch of the imagination and secondly, I couldn't come to terms with the fact that God actually wanted me to do something.

I read the verse a couple of more times and told my wife what I thought had just happened. I sensed that God wanted me to go down to my local shopping centre and tell people about Jesus. Well you could imagine how thrilled I was about that. I couldn't even order over the counter at the city market for the fear of the face of man. However I knew somehow that I had to go and do this thing for the Lord. I knew that it was the voice of the Holy Spirit leading me, something I will talk more about in the next chapter.

With a great deal of natural fear and embarrassment I went out and bought fifty dollars worth of tracts and began giving them out at our local shopping centre. It was pretty big with a large number of shops and several corridors leading in different directions from a central point, which was a large open area with a few seats and an information counter etc. As I began to distribute the tracts, I would hand one to someone and say if you would like to talk about what's in the tract I will be around in the shops for some time. That's all I could think to say and that was hard enough especially with some of the comments I was getting being less than encouraging.

Even though I was afraid to start with, I felt as though I wasn't alone, but that God was with me. I had not experienced that the same way before. I survived the day and shortly after, I was offered an opportunity to speak to a group of high school students in an organized meeting. I asked the Lord If I should do it and to my surprise He answered me in the same way I had heard that inner voice telling me to go to the shop. While I was preparing my talk I began to get an idea where this thing was going and I thought no way. I had a picture in my mind of being called to preach and teach. I know what the scripture said, but I thought I could talk my way out of it with God because of my fear. I told God it was no good calling me because I couldn't talk to hardly anybody let alone preach, so I set about proving it. I took a travel clock from my room and put it on the table in front of me, of course we have clocks, internet, music, blue tooth, and all other sorts of thing right in our phones these days. Well I put this clock on the table in front of me and proceeded to show God that I couldn't even talk for five minutes.

Each time I started to talk I would go for about a minute and get stuck. I said to God, "I'll go and talk but I'm not confident at all". I was really nervous on the day and I had a paper with things written down on it that I could read.

It went ok and the people said that I should talk again the following week because they said they felt it came from my heart.

The following week came but this time instead of telling God I couldn't do it I prayed and asked Him what I should speak about. I can't remember the topic now but what I do remember is that He said to me, "I don't want you to use written notes this time". I knew

God wanted me to trust Him so I did, and just made a brief outline of about four points and let God fill in the gaps.

You might wonder why I'm sharing this story, well it wasn't long before I felt to accept in prayer the responsibility of the calling God had called me to so I prayed like this.

"Father I accept that you have called me to the ministry and I accept your Word that says my sufficiency is of you not of myself, so I'm trusting you God because I don't feel very special or righteous, but I believe your Word and you said I am, and I can, so ok". From that time on I began to see the image inside of me of the kind of person that I wanted to be. I have confessed God's word over my life and that of my family ever since and the more I followed, the more I learned about what I have and what I can do, and the more I believed for it and confessed it the better everything to do with ministry life became. Today I have the ability to stand before anybody and any amount of numbers and declare the saving grace of our Lord and Savior. I've spoken and given counsel to people of all walks of life from little children to politicians, from little old ladies to hardened criminals. I was able to do this for the Lord at his request, because of the picture I developed on the inside of myself. It's a picture that the Word of God paints by telling us who we are in Christ.

> **8. "This book of the law shall not depart out of your mouth; but thou shalt meditate therein day and night, that thou mayest observe to do according to all that is written therein: for then thou shalt make thy way prosperous, and then thou shalt have good success." (Josh. 1 v 8)**

You see staying in God's Word and continually reading who we are in Christ, continually observing what is to be followed and believed for, will ensure that the inner image or picture of you in your future will be one of power and success, guided by God Himself. I'm not talking about mind power here, as in we think of something and then think it into being. I'm talking about a plan, an idea born in the heart of God, powered by the love of God in His Word, and carried out by the ministry of the Holy Spirit in the Earth. Let me show you the difference.

> **29. "By faith they passed through the Red sea as by dry land: which the Egyptians as saying to do were drowned." (Heb. 11 v 29)**

You see the Israelites passed through the Red Sea because they were operating in faith based on a promise of God to deliver them from their captors of four hundred years. The Egyptians however said basically, "if they can do it so can we", and they set off after them between the waters which were held back by God because of the faith of Moses. When God's people were through to the other side the waters fell back into their natural position and the Egyptians were drowned. You see they had no covenant with God, no agreement that God would deliver them, and so they were drowned. They were an example of people today thinking their money or their good looks or their street smarts will be enough to see them through, but just as the Egyptians found, they also will find, that unless the picture on the inside of you, telling you what you can do is of God based on His promises, you have no guarantee of success. All the money in the world and all the boldness you can muster will not save you from a terminal illness if you don't have a heart full of the word of God. Frame the picture of your life with words of faith in God's promises that He has spoken over you. God's Word is a living thing, He has the power to bring itself to pass, it's full of the energy and life of God; the Zoe' life; the power that makes God who He is. In **Marks Gospel chapter four** we read;

> **15. "And these are they by the wayside, where the word is sown; but when they have heard, satin cometh immediately, and taketh away the seed that was sown in their hearts." (Mk. 4 v 15)**

You've probably heard or read for yourselves this scripture before in the contexts of, forgetting what it says after you read it. I want you to think of it telling you that satan immediately comes to steal, not just the word, but the inner image that the word has just created in you. Whatever you hear from the Word of God will to some degree build you up in an area, it will add another brick in the wall of the picture of invincibility, competency and sufficiency that is developing inside you, and that is dangerous to the devil.

If he can get that word out of your mind before it takes root and develops faith all the better for him. Remember James tells us that not acting on the word will cause us to forget what we have read, so the more we meditate on it, think about it and act on it daily, the deeper it goes in our spirit and the harder it is for satan to get us off it.

Romans tells us that death reigned because of one man, by Adam, and that grace now reigns because of one man, by Jesus.

17. "For if by one man's offence death reigned by one; much more they which receive abundance of grace and of the gift of righteousness shall reign in life by one, Jesus Christ." (Rom. 5 v 17)

satan is afraid of the revelation you have in regard to your righteousness because the Bible says you will reign. To reign means to be king or Queen, to exercise the highest influence, to control. satan is terrified you are going to realize just who you are in Christ. He's terrified that the inner image is going to grow so big that it burst out all over everything you touch and are involved in with faith and determination, and just rip into the strong holds that he has had in and over people's lives. Next time the devil asks who do you think you are? Tell him, say; "I'm a reborn, recreated, Spirit filled, Word believing, blessing, creative, power house of God's love, and I'm not going to allow you any territory in my life or the life of my family and friends, in the name of Jesus Christ of Nazareth get away from my family, friends, my business, my church and get your hands of my money".

Let God's Word be the paint and the Holy Spirit be the Artist, and let them create your inner image. Then speak out the image you have within you and see it transform your life. The devil told a lie but we're not going to believe it anymore right?

About a year after I started to teach, I was teaching on the authority the believers have in the Earth. One night my room became very cold, so I put all the covers I had at the time on the bed. I was still cold, so I put a track suit on as well. I couldn't believe how cold my room was. At some point in the night I awoke and felt a strange intensity in my room. Then suddenly, I felt a huge pair of hands grab me on both sides of my rib cage. I can't describe how much of a fright that was, especially since at thirty three I was still uneasy in the dark, a legacy of my unsupported childhood. I knew immediately that it was an evil presence, and all I could manage because I was totally pinned to the bed, and my mouth stretched tight at the sides, was to say the name of Jesus. At first the name didn't come out properly, but eventually I could say the name clearly and loud. When I did the presence eased off and I could stand. I stood there shouting all the scriptures on dominion and authority I could think of, and chased that entity (that demonic force) out off my house and life for good. As I said, up to that time I had still been afraid of the dark. After that night I would get up and sit in the dark and say now the dark belongs to me. I would get up and just sit there and mock the devil because he is defeated, and I would do it on purpose. I have never been afraid to be in a dark place since. The inner image I have now is one of authority and accomplishment in Christ, as should yours be, **it's God's will to do it for you.**

Chapter Nine

Be led By the Holy Spirit

> 16. "And I will pray the Father, and he shall give you another comforter, that he may abide with you forever;"
>
> 17. "Even the Spirit of truth; whom the world cannot receive, because it seeth him not, neither knoweth him: but ye know him; for he dwelleth with you, and shall be in you."(Jn. 14 v 16-17)

WHEN JESUS' TIME came to be offered up on the Alter of the Cross by the High Priest, as the sacrificial Lamb of God for the sins of the world, He knew we would be in deep trouble again, if we didn't have someone to help us. Once He had come amongst us He wanted to stay with us, but He could as a man, only be in one place at any given time. As well as this, He had to face the cross, go into hell and then ascend into heaven to sprinkle the heavenly utensils of worship with his blood. This then called for another strategy, so he said, "I will ask God when I go away to send the Holy Spirit to you to help you, so you will always have God with you".

The Amplified Bible says it this way;

> 16. "And I will ask the Father, and He will send the comforter (counselor, helper, Intercessor, Advocate, Strengthener, and Standby) that he may remain with you forever."(Jn.14 v16) Amp.

God did send us the Holy Spirit as the Apostle Paul tells us that;

15. "For ye have not received the spirit of bondage again to fear; but ye have received the Spirit of adoption, whereby we cry, Abba Father." (Rom. 8 v 15)

That word Abba is a word like our word Daddy. Father is traditionally the responsible head of the family, but Daddy is the one we jump all over when were playing. That's something that's not taught a lot in churches that God is our Daddy not just Father, He'll rejoice with us, be happy and joyful and singing with us, as well as be directional and instructive. You might like to spend some time considering that thought.

God is intimately interested in our lives and He is only too pleased to fellowship and spend time with us, going through the days that make up our lives. Some people find that concept a hard thing to come to terms with. It maybe because their idea of a father figure is not the best picture for some people or that they have never considered themselves someone that God would be interested enough in personally, to actually spend time with; after all he is busy looking after everyone in the whole world and why would he be interested in me or my prayers when he's so busy?

Well He is, if you were the only person on the earth Jesus still would have come, and gone to the cross to save you. Now that's an awesome thought isn't it? The reason He sent his Spirit to be with us, was for that very reason He cares enough to want us to be looked after, and we can if we learn to listen and be led by the Spirit of God in all that we do. You can see how that would be a recipe for success in anybody's book. I have long ago said to God that He is welcome to show me things or interrupt me anytime He thinks I need instruction, or to ask me to do something for Him. I was at home one day and the Spirit of the Lord spoke up on the inside of me and said "go and get a haircut". I said "Lord I only had a haircut two days ago". As if He didn't already know that. About a minute later I heard him say it again "go and get a haircut". I said "ok Lord I'll "Go over to the shops right now and get a haircut". I arrived at the shop, went in and sat down. It was a female hairdresser and she was giving a lady something that required her to have some rollers in her hair, while another woman was in the seat next to me waiting for her turn. Again the Spirit of the Lord spoke to me in my mind and said "I want you to get her saved". I was very nervous about this it seemed a strange way of doing it. Never the less I said "Ok Lord but you're going to have to do something about the customers". Just then the woman next to me got up and left the shop, saying she would return in a minute. Shortly after, the woman in the chair said, "Oh golly, I just remembered I was supposed to do something" that I didn't quite catch, with that, she got out of the chair, took out the few curlers that were in her hair and hurried off. I was pretty amazed, but what happened next was even more amazing. In my mind I thought, ok but you're going to have to lock the door or someone else will come in. Just then a woman tried the door and it was as though locked. She just walked away. With that the hairdresser looked at me and said "Well I guess your next then". I stood up and walked to the chair and said to the woman, (whose name I discovered later was Michelle) that, "I didn't really come here for a haircut but that God had sent me to get you saved". With that she began to cry and told me that she had been praying, that someone would lead her in the way of salvation. I prayed with her and arranged some follow up counselling with her and left. Needless to say I got my hair cut for free there as long as she had the shop.

You see God knows what it takes. I received a lesson in trusting the inner voice of the Holy Spirit and the woman had an encounter with the Love of God Everything God does benefits everybody involved. God's leading always creates a win, win situation.

6. "In all thy ways acknowledge him, and he shall direct your paths."(Prov.3v6)

Learning to follow the leading of the Holy Spirit's voice is not only satisfying but exciting. There is another aspect of the Holy Spirits leading that some Christians don't avail themselves of, and that is in relation to your prayer life;

20. "But ye beloved, building up yourselves on your most holy faith, praying in the Holy Ghost." (Jude.V20)

The Bible encourages us to pray in many ways, pray without ceasing, ask and you shall receive, pray in the Holy Ghost as here, to pray with supplication and thanks giving, to pray in faith nothing wavering, pray for the sick, and so on. There are a couple of special jobs though that the Holy Spirit does for us when we pray.

One is that as Jude tells us here, is to build us up. When we pray in the Holy Ghost or in the Spirit as we say, we pray using our prayer tongue language or praying in tongues, and by doing so we edify or build ourselves up. We become stronger mentally and more confident because it takes faith to pray in tongues. A lot of Christians won't pray in tongues because they believe that it's from the devil.

Jesus said a house divided against its self can't stand, so if the **(1Cor.14v15)** Bible and ministries that are getting people saved healed and delivered advocate praying in the Spirit, I think that it's safe to do so. The fact is that you recognize in your own spirit that it is God. The reason people think it's from the devil is because they themselves haven't received the baptism of the Holy Spirit which is different than having the Spirit of God come in your spirit when you are saved; and the tongues are the physical evidence that that the baptism has taken place that the gift has been received.

Apart from this the Bible tells us that;

> **26. "Likewise the Spirit also helpeth our infirmities: for we know not what we should pray for as we ought: but the Spirit itself maketh intersession for us with groaning which cannot be uttered." (Rom.8 v 26)**

Notice that it says helpeth. Well that word we've translated helpeth in our language is a much better promise in the Greek from where it came. It says that the Spirit takes hold together with us to help us in the areas of weakness or where we lack understanding.

God has his Spirit come along side us, support us, counsel with us, strengthen us, guide us and if you will accept it, gives us the words to pray in our prayer language. This not only covers that which we should say, but says it in a way that is perfectly acceptable to God. He helps us, the Bible says, for we know not what we should pray. So in fact when you pray in the Spirit, guided by Him, you pray the perfect prayer to your Heavenly Father. That ought to give you confidence that He will answer your prayers. The Bible tells us to pray in the Spirit and with understanding **Romans fourteen verse fifteen**, so when you are praying for something and you're not sure where to go with it, not sure exactly what needs doing, you can avail yourself of the ministry of the Holy Spirit and pray in the Spirit, your prayer being guided by Him to the Father.

I was director of a ministry in the eighties called Proclaim Evangelical Ministries it was a Teaching and Evangelical Ministry which held meetings in High Schools as well as other activities, like Nursing Home Visitation with a view to bringing the Gospel to people before we lost them for good, and providing speakers for other organizations, such as the Full Gospel Business Men's groups and Churches etc.

Each morning at six o'clock I would start our day with a prayer meeting, with whoever was there in attendance. One morning while I was praying, I had a strong urge to declare a day of prayer, so I told everyone concerned and sent the request out to all of our prayer warriors, those people that supported our ministry with prayer, able bodied and financial support, that I was declaring a day of prayer. It wasn't until about two weeks after the day that I received word from another ministry we were partnered with in the U.S.A., because of mail delays that they were encouraging us to set aside a day of prayer with them. It turned out that it was the same day we had declared and we had prayed about the same things they had asked be included. Being awake and alert to the voice of the Holy Spirit will keep you on track with everything in your life.

Some people today still rely on the ministry of the prophet to lead them in their lives, but the Bible teaches that we are to be led by the Spirit, not prophecy. There is a place for the prophet today, but it's not to lead the children of God in their personal lives. If it stays in the realm of edification, exhortation or comfort, and confirming something you believe God has told you then its ok.

15. "For as many as are led by the Spirit of God they are the children of God." (Rom. 8 v 14)

If someone gives you what they believe is a word from the Lord for you in your situation, or a direction to take in your life for the future, it must align with something that God has already put across your thinking. That way it will confirm to you (as the Bible says in the mouth of two or more witnesses let a thing be established) **(11Cor. 13 v 1)** what God has told you to do or that you were thinking God wants you to do etc. and instead of leading you in the first instance. If it is the first time you've thought or heard of a suggestion and it comes from someone telling you it's from God, you should put it on the shelf and ask God to confirm it to you. If He doesn't confirm it clearly to you take no further notice of the suggestion. Remember the children of God are led by the Spirit of God, nowhere does it say that we are to be led by prophecy or by the prophet. Those days are gone with the old dispensation, with the Old Testament. **Romans eight verse 16** tells us that;

16. "The Spirit itself beareth witness with our spirit, that we are the children of God;"

You see the Spirit of God will reside inside you and bear witness with your own spirit, in other words you will have a knowing in your being that God wants you to do or go or say etc. just as I did with the Hairdresser for example.

Remember Jesus said He will come and be our helper and our guide, the devil will try to lead you astray if he can so you miss God's best, so don't let him. If you live in the Word so you know what God has said about something and then allow yourself to be led by the Spirit, you will have good success.

We often hear people talking about conscience. What they are actually talking about is the voice of their spirit, as opposed to the Holy Spirit, it's more of a perception than a voice. You know yourself if you do wrong you have a sense that you really shouldn't have done that, or if you do well you have a sense of well done, even though you don't hear a voice. That's your spirit man communicating with your mind.

The Bible tells us;

27." The spirit of a man is the candle of the Lord........."

Our spirit man is indwelt by the Holy Spirit it's that Spirit that quickened us from the dead at the command of the Lord when we accepted Christ as our Savior. Because our spirit is indwelt it can be guided by the Fathers, and as the scripture says becomes a candle showing our way. We will receive direction in our spirit man not in our head, but the spirit will communicate it to our mind so as we can act upon it. In the Book of Romans Paul tells us;

10. "And said unto them, Sirs I perceive that this voyage will be with hurt and much damage not only of the lading and ship, but also of our lives." (Acts. 27 v 10)

Notice that Paul perceived it, he didn't say God told me, he didn't say he heard a voice, he said he perceived it, or sensed it in his spirit, and then he conveyed his concerns to the crew so as to warn them of danger.

I was on bus one day going to the city, when I noticed a woman with a little boy, and I sensed The Holy Spirit wanted me to talk to her. I really didn't know why, but I just went ahead and said hello and struck up a conversation about looking after children.

We spoke for a while and then got off the bus. She had told me where she lived and it turned out to be just around the corner from me. The next time I saw her she was on our local beach sunbathing topless, just as I said "Hi" the Holy Spirit said "talk to her awhile and don't be embarrassed". I sat down with her and we just talked as though there were nothing out of the ordinary. She told me she thought an Evangelist was some kind of Bikie, and how she was annoyed by the men that hang around to see her topless, and other such things.

While I was at my desk the next day this woman came to my mind, so I asked the Lord if there was a reason for that. Then the Spirit of God said to me to go and give her fifty dollars because she needs it.

I took the money around to her house and knocked at the door. When she answered I saw two men in the house, and they along with this young lady were having a few drinks etc. When I saw the drink and cigarettes etc the devil jumped straight into my mind with, you got it wrong, besides she'll only waste it on booze and drugs. For one brief second I hesitated, and then said, "God told me to come and give you this money". She said, "thanks "and shut the door. I had thought in that moment of pause, that I was asked to give it to her not to judge the situation, and so I gave her the money as the Lord had instructed me to.

You see if your faith is in God and not circumstance even If you were wrong God would bless your giving because it's a Bible principal to sow and reap. I didn't see her for a few days and the whole time the devil was in my ear telling me she just wasted the money. When I did see her again she told me she was so grateful for the money, the guys that were there that day had apparently just turned up for a visit uninvited and began drinking. She told me that she had been able to buy food for herself and her little boy with the money, as she was out of cash at the time. As a consequence of my following the leading of the Holy Spirit over a couple of weeks I was able to lead her in a prayer for her salvation. You see God knows what it takes to get a situation working for everyone's good. In this case I was now going to receive for my giving, the prayer warriors were going to be blessed because they share in the ministry blessings because they pray and give, and the young lady was now a child of God. You see if I'd been worried about my reputation on the beach and not stopped or if I had judged the situation in her flat when I took her the money and just kept it, or not spoken to her on the bus as I felt that unction to do, this whole scenario would probably have been different and she may not be saved today.

Never be afraid to follow the leading of the Holy Spirit because you fear what people may think. Remember Jesus fellowshipped with some real characters to get them into the kingdom.

One sunny morning I was feeling good about most things and decided to walk to the bank, and enjoy some fresh air to take care of some business. While I was in the bank I noticed one of the tellers, she just seemed to stand out to me I smiled as she looked my way and didn't really think anything of it. The next time I went to the bank she was the teller that served me. After I had been home for a while I received a phone call from her. She asked me to forgive her and not say anything but she had broken the rules and looked up my file to get my phone number, because as she said, "there was something special, something different about me," she said I was bright as if a light was shining in me and she wanted to know what it was. I explained to her that it was the light of God the light of the Holy Spirit in me that she was seeing. The Bible says that God is light and that we are the light to the world.

This lady explained to me after a little discussion and questioning both ways that she went to church, but had never actually been saved, she had never as an adult accepted Jesus as her Lord and savior. God knows more than we do He knows the best way to get things done, all we have to do is trust that he knows what's best for our everyday lives, and things get much easier. I did some garden work for an old fellow one day, and when I had finished he said "What do I owe you"? I said "Don't worry about it", so he replied, "Well can I do something for you"? Just then I heard Spirit say, "Tell him he can give his life to Jesus", so I did and he looked stunned for a second, and then said, "Ok I will".

At a nursing home that I visited regularly in the eighties, there was an old German fellow who had been in the war, and I suspect from conversations with him that he had done some things that were not all that kind. He had little time for anybody and no time for me when I first approached him. His name was Fred, and old Fred was about as bigger grump as I had ever met. I would stop in on Fred and share about Jesus and his love and forgiveness and Fred would say to me "I don believe nuting, dus good food unt good drrrink unt das it" So each time I would pass his door I would ask "What do you believe Fred"? And each time I would get the same answer good food etc.

I asked the Lord "How or what do I need to get through to the guy"? While I was praying about our visitation program the Spirit of God showed me a picture in my mind about the fruit trees spoken of that are in heaven. I really couldn't see the relevance to Fred's case but I took God's advice and the leading of the Holy Spirit and went to talk to Fred about the food in heaven. I can't remember the conversation now but the outcome was that Fred gave his heart to the Lord and accepted Christ Jesus as his savior. From then on as I passed his door I would ask what do you believe Fred? He would reply, "I believe in good food unt good drrrink unt Jesus"! Shortly afterwards Fred passed away. God knew what it would take to get Fred saved, the Holy Spirit led me to talk to a bitter man about something that I thought was Irrelevant. If you learn to hear and trust the leading of the Holy Spirit you will always have an answer and He will always show you a way.

> **16. "..........for ye are the temple of the living God; as God hath said, I will dwell in them; and I will be their God, and they shall be my people." (11Cor. 6 v 16)**

God has given us his word that he is living in us. God who created all things resides on the inside of you in your spirit man. You see you are a spirit, you live inside a body and you have a mind, which makes up your emotions, your intellect and your will. The Bible says that "He who is joined to the lord is one spirit". You are one spirit with God **(1Cor 6 v 17)**. This vessel or body we posses, cannot live when the spirit leaves, it just stops working. It's the spirit or the heart of a man as the Bible calls it, as in the centre, like the heart of a tree, not the blood pump that keeps it alive.

The Bible tells us that;

> **7. "But we have this treasure in earthen vessels, that the excellency of the power may be of God, and not of us." (11Cor. 4 v 7)**

God that commanded the light to shine out of the darkness, has shined in our hearts to give the light of the knowledge of the glory of God in the face of Jesus Christ **(11Cor. 4 v 6)**. In other words we have this glory, the power of God, that creative energy, the Zoe' life of God that makes God who He is, in this earthen vessel we call a body. He is living in here with us and the more we develop faith in that fact, the more we will begin to step out fearlessly just as Jesus did in his earthly ministry. He is in us because He's for us He wants us to be a vessel for the masters use so He can work through us.

I was walking home one evening when I was much younger, when a car load of guys started abusing me. I ignored it for a while, but I wasn't as patient then as I am now and I began to get angry inside. I noticed that the car had stopped at the traffic lights about fifty meters further on. I was so angry that I started to run to catch up with them before the light changed. I had spent a good deal of my youth fighting and I felt rage coming up inside, I really didn't care at that moment if I got hurt as long as I could punish the driver who had done most of the talking. The Lord has since delivered me of that murderous angry spirit, but at the time I was fired up and Just as I started to run the Spirit of the Lord said to me "What did the Word say about praying for people like this "? I said, "But Lord these guys need punishing", but I could feel the pressure to do the right thing. I said, "He said I should pray for them".

Then He said "Then kneel down and pray for them". I said "but that's just like rubbing salt into the wound, they abuse me and I have to pray for them". I just couldn't get my head or my heart around this thing and God seemed to be so insistent about it. Well by this time the car had gone but I was still eaten up inside with anger over the whole incident.

I finally did what God had asked me to do and I kneeled down on the footpath next to a pretty busy road and prayed honestly for those guys. I didn't care what anybody driving past thought I wanted to obey my Lord. Immediately I felt the anger leave as soon as I forgave those guys the anger and the agitation went from me. I couldn't believe how I could feel so angry one second, and not the next. You see God wasn't trying to rub salt into the wound or trying to punish or humiliate me for being angry, He knew that when I forgave, the pressure the devil was pushing me with would ease, and that leverage would be gone from my mind.

> **44. "But I say unto you, love your enemies and bless them that curse you, do good to them that hate you, and pray for them that despitefully use you, and persecute you;"**

> **45. "That ye may be the children of your Father which is in Heaven: for he maketh his sun to rise on the evil and on the good, and sendeth rain on the just and the unjust." (Matt. 5 v 44-45)**

I learned a valuable lesson that day and was never troubled in the same way again.

The Spirit of God is also called our strengthener, Paul the Apostle prayed that we might be strong in the Lord, and in the power of his might (**Eph.6v10**). The Holy Spirit has come to strengthen us in our walk with God. He will empower your with Gods power to overcome pressures and He will help you develop your inner Strength, (your character), so as you can resist temptation in the day of trouble.

Paul tells us that we should know how to posses our vessel, or body with honor,

> 4 "That every one of you should know how to posses his vessel in sanctification and honour." (1 Thess. 4v4)

God wants us to posses the vessel this body that is filled with the glory of God, filled with the Holy Spirit of God, in such a way that we are willingly separated from the world and its ways of operating. Having a sense of the righteousness that God through Christ has imparted to us, and to conduct ourselves as ministers of the New Testament, the Gospel of life and peace: and the way to do that is to be led by the Spirit in all we do. God wants us to be successful that's why the Spirit was given to guide us. It's God's will that it happen for you.

Now a lot of people still think that the Baptism of the Holy Spirit is the same as receiving the Spirit at the new birth. Let's just clarify that a little because God is not a God of confusion.

> 5. "Then Philip went down to the city of Sa-mar-i-a and preached Christ to them."

> 12 "But when they believed Philip preaching the things concerning the kingdom of God, and the name of Jesus Christ, they were baptized, both men and women."

> 14 "Now when the Apostles which were at Jerusalem heard that Samaria had received the word of God, they sent Peter and John:"

> 15. "Who when they were come prayed that may receive the Holy Ghost:"
>
> 16. "(For as yet He was fallen on none of them: only they were baptized in the name of the Lord Jesus)."
>
> 17. "Then they laid their hands on them, and they received the Holy Ghost." (Acts. 8 v 5, 12, 14-17).

The Christian that is born again has been given the Spirit of God which now resides in his spirit; and by this act of God's grace has received the energizing power of life into his spirit. Whereas before his spirit was dead to God and headed for incarceration with the evil ones at the time of judgment, he is now a Child of God and will live forever with Him.

You can see from the scriptures that being baptized into Christ left something still to be received, that the Apostles went to Samaria to impart to these new converts by the laying on of their hands.

Paul asked the disciples he came across at Ephesus if they had received the Holy Ghost since they had believed, and they answered him that they didn't even know there was a Holy Ghost **(Acts. 19 v 2)**. Now these people were as saved as the next person they professed their belief in Christ as lord and had received the Holy Ghost at their conversion. The Bible says that no man calls Jesus the Lord but by the Holy Spirit. **(1Cor. 12 v 3)** Paul however shows us here again that there is some other thing to be had in relation to the Spirit of God;

> 6. "And when Paul had laid his hands upon them, the Holy Ghost came on them; the Holy Ghost came on them; and they spake with tongues, and prophesied." (Acts 19 v 6).

Here again, as I've mentioned before, is the sign of receiving the Baptism of the Holy Ghost (as being different to receiving Him at the moment of the new birth), in that these people then began speaking with other tongues as the Spirit gave them utterance. If it were the same thing there would have been no need for Peter or Paul to lay hands on them to receive after they had believed.

Let's have a look at another example of proof of what I'm saying, but this time the other way round. When we check out a math equation we often do it in reverse to see if the numbers still prove out our answer, so let's apply that principal here.

We've seen how after receiving Jesus as Lord there was a need to be filled or baptized in the Holy Spirit. Well here we can see that after being filled with the Spirit there was another baptism needed;

> **44. "While Peter yet spake these words, the Holy Ghost fell on all them which heard the word."**
>
> **45. "And they of the circumcision which believed were astonished, as many as came with Peter, because that on the Gentiles also was poured out the gift of the Holy Ghost.**
>
> **46. "For they heard them speak with tongues, and magnified God. Then answered Peter,"**
>
> **47. "Can any man forbid water, that these should not be baptized, which have received the Holy Ghost as well as we**
>
> **48. "And he commanded them to be baptized in the name of the Lord. Then prayed they him to tarry certain days." (Acts 10 v 44-48)**

We see how God baptized these people in the Holy Ghost and spoke in tongues. Peter then said they needed to be baptized into Christ with water, which would have been done on the confession of their faith that they had received Him as Lord. So we can see from these scriptures that there are two different infillings of the Spirit, and two different baptisms.

The reason we need the infilling or the Baptism of the Holy Spirit as differing from that of salvation can be found in the first chapter of Acts.

In the first chapter of Act we read;

> **5. "For John truly baptized with water; but ye shall be baptized with the Holy Ghost not many days hence."**
>
> **8. "But ye shall receive power after that the Holy Ghost has come upon you: and ye shall be witnesses unto me both in Jerusalem, and in all Judaea, and in Samaria and unto the utter most part of the Earth." (Acts. 1 v 5+8)**

Jesus here first of all makes the distinction between Water and Holy Ghost Baptism, and then goes on to say that because of this baptism coming upon them they would receive power. The word used here and translated power is the word Dunamis. It's the word we get our word dynamo from it means literally miracle power, the power to do miracles. When the Bible talks about the power to become the children, or the sons of God, the word translated power there is the word Exousia, which means the authority, or the right to become.

You see when you were born into the earth of a woman (as Jesus was and devils can't be), it gives you the right to have dominion in the earth, your body is your badge of authority in the world. This right is not exercised because man lost his authority, his Exousia power to the devil in the Garden. Jesus however, bought, won and took this power back for us when He beat satan in Hell, and then gave back to us the power and rights that God intended man to have in the first place.

When a person is born again he becomes a new creature in Christ and he has rights in the earth over sin, sickness and poverty, and all the works of evil. However, enforcing those rights is often difficult because we have an adversary in the devil. He will oppose everything we do because he hates us, and he hates us because we are children of God, and he isn't, he's just an outlaw in the Earth. The purpose of the Baptism or the infilling of the Holy Spirit is to empower you. Jesus told them to tarry or wait for the Holy Ghost to come upon them because he knew that when a person is baptized in the Holy Ghost he is baptized with the power to do miracles. He is empowered to undo everything the devil means for evil. Jesus walked in the Earth as a man in a man's body, exercising a man's authority to resist sin. He walked in the Earth with incredible power because He was anointed. This anointing comes, Jesus tells us here in Acts, after the Holy Ghost has come upon you. He said they would receive Dunamis power Dynamite power the power to face any obstacle the devil could throw at them and come out victorious, because they had the power of God. They had the same power to use that Jesus used to heal the sick, cast out devils and to calm the storm. Hallelujah! We can police the devil in our and others lives, and still the storms of life with the power of God on the inside of us.

I was sharing with a woman in my home one day who had come because her husband had said to her that "she needs to come and see me, and get God in her life", because he felt that He (God) would help her a lot. I thought this to be a little ironic as the man himself didn't ever like me talking about God around him. He just thought he was too bad to receive God's blessing of salvation himself, but believed his partner could. So she was here talking to me. I gave her some literature and just as I handed it to her the Holy ghost said to me to "Tell her if she has trouble reading it that you'll pray about her eyes", so I did just that, I repeated what I'd heard the Spirit say to me in the inner voice. When I said it she looked startled at me and said "how did you know I had bad eyes"? I said "I didn't but God does and He just told me". So I prayed in relation to her sight and she left happy.

The reason the Spirit of God is in the earth is to be a helper and guide, so He will guide us, to help others as need. So too the gifts of the Spirit spoken of in chapter twelve of first Corinthians, I won't go into that teaching in this book at this time but suffice to say they are given to us to profit it says, every man with all. God given gifts are for everybody to profit or receive assistance by. **God's will is to do it for you**, to see that we receive Help, Guidance, Comfort, Strength, Counsel, Advocacy and an Intercessor.

Chapter Ten

Grace to Help

**"Let us therefore come boldly
unto the throne of Grace,"**

**"That we may obtain mercy, and find
Grace to help in time of need."**

THE TITLE OF this book is that it is God's will is to do it for you, well to do what? Whatever you need!

As the scripture verse above tells us, we are to come to God's throne to get help if we need it. If you didn't want to help someone would you say come over and I'll help you? No of course you wouldn't. Well God's no different, He wouldn't say come for help if He didn't mean it. Not only does He say "come" but He says "come boldly". If you were to ask for something boldly of someone, it would denote that you thought you had a right to it. If this then is the case, God must consider that a deserving attitude is ok. What would allow us, and have God to think, that we deserve to come boldly and say what it is we need. Jesus of course! His sacrifice and substitution for us is what's bought us the right. We always come with thanks giving for what Jesus has done, and to God for his goodness toward us, but that's a different thing. Coming to God boldly and with confidence of the answer is what Jesus died to buy back for us; the right standing with God the Father. Righteousness means in right standing or in favor in the right place of acceptance. Grace is literally the unmerited or undeserved favor of God. In other words we don't deserve it on the basis of anything we've done it's a free gift on the basis of Jesus' sacrifice on our behalf.

This whole thing is God's Grace, salvation, blessings of every kind, healings, provision, instruction, love, the name of Jesus, the Blood of the Lamb, everything to do with God, and this earth, it's all due to the Grace of God. Grace is love, God is love, and God's Grace is to show His love. The story of the Gospel is the story of Grace. We earn nothing by works lest we boast, after all our righteousness is as filthy rags the Bible says. (And by the way if you study it out, they're menstrual rags it's talking about). We offer God nothing He's interested in when we think we're being good to earn favour, but there are still people and church organizations that teach that we must keep Sabbaths and rules of every kind to gain favor and acceptance from God. What a self righteous attitude, to think we could actually impress God with what we have to offer outside of Grace.

James tells us to show our faith in our works but that's a different thing. That means we need to act on our faith in the work of Christ, having faith in what Jesus has done and then living and acting accordingly to bring a result.

Romans the fifth chapter tells us that we are at peace with God being justified by faith in Jesus Christ:

2. "By whom also we have access by faith into this Grace wherein we stand, and rejoice in hope of the Glory of God." (Rom. 5 v 2)

The very position we stand in waiting for the Glory of God to manifest in us when our mortal shall be changed to immortal is only available because of the Grace God extends to us through Jesus Christ. In **Acts chapter four verse thirty three** it says that great grace was upon the people and because of that, they brought their positions and money and sold land etc. and brought the wealth to the Apostles feet to be distributed to whoever needed it. When God's grace fell upon them they became generous and wanted to willingly help those in need. That's the Grace of God in action that's the benevolence of God He is a giving loving Father and when he gets on us we become the same. The Grace of God is the benevolence the true heart of God in action. Undeserved but given anyway. Notice it didn't say in Acts that those who were worthy it said those that had need.

> **32. "And now, brethren, I commend you to God, and to the word of his grace, which is able to build you up, and to give you an inheritance among all them which are sanctified." (Acts 20 v 32)**

He again we see the benevolence or the Grace of God His Word it says is able to build us up make us strong teach us how to be over comers, and to give us an inheritance of eternal life and life more abundant while we're here while separating us from those that are not Gods.

He's always giving, always organizing things around benefiting us the jewel in his crown of creation, always providing, healing and blessing, always operating with GRACE. We're told to fear God in the Bible, but this word translated fear means to respect and honor. That's one of the problems with our language compared to the Greek for instance. It can be quite ambiguous at times.

> **29. "Let no corrupt communication proceed out of your mouth, but that which is good to the use of edifying, that it may minister grace to the hearers."**

> **30. "And grieve not the Holy Spirit of God, whereby ye are sealed unto the day of redemption."**

> **31. Let all bitterness, and wrath, and anger, and clamour, and evil speaking, be put away from you, with all malice:"**

> **32. "And be ye kind one to another, tenderhearted, forgiving one another, even as God for Christ's sake hath forgiven you."**

God encourages us here to be as He is and operate in grace, speaking only useful, kind words that build people up, and not pull them down. That's the way God is, so when people prophesy that God says He's going to punish you or some other negative comment toward you or others, you can say with assurance, "that statement is not of God". God has forgiven us for Christ's sake He has extended to us the grace of forgiveness which we did not deserve.

When you have a revelation of the grace of God, you can truly rest from your works and trust the Word of God believing the promises, and know that you are accepted of Him for yourself. You no longer need to have that element of doubt and twinges of fear that you may be out of favor because of some minor infraction. Then you can truly begin to experience the peace that passes all understanding. What that means is that it passes or is hard to understand with our natural minds thinking. It is understood though by our spirit man, it's a peace that is assurance and contentment, an acceptance in our own mind that God loves us and cares for us and keeps us in his love in His Grace. No matter whom you are or what you've done.**"Let us come boldly to the throne of Grace"**. You see it is a Grace Throne, its Gods Throne, the King's Throne, the Lords Throne, the Creator's Throne; it's the throne representing the most power, the most honour, the most creative throne that ever was, that is, or ever will be in this universe, or the one to come. It's the throne of Grace, the Grace throne. It's what the Throne of God is all about, "Grace". That one word encapsulates all that is God, all that God has ever done, and all the reason behind it. It is what God is all about "Grace". It's His love, kindness, caring, giving, and mindfulness of you and I personally, it's His Grace.

God's Grace affords us our life and everything we've been promised by Him. One person described the word Grace, to be "God's Riches At Christ's Expense" **God's will** (and His good pleasure) **is to do it for you**. So be blessed.

Chapter Eleven

First the Blade
The Law of Patient Progression

26. "And he said, so is the kingdom of God, as if a man should cast seed into the ground;"

27. "And should sleep, and rise night and day, and the seed should spring and grow up, he knows not how."

28. "For the Earth bringeth forth fruit of herself; first the blade, then the ear, after that the full corn in the ear."

29. "But when the fruit is brought forth, immediately he putteth in the sickle, because the harvest is come."

WE'VE SEEN HOW God will give to us, and that it's his good pleasure, as well as his idea in the first place. We've also looked at why he feels that He wants to give us good things and to love us. How we are to receive, by using our faith, and just what that faith is and how to release it to be most effective. Further to this we have seen how God's Word is to be relied upon, because of the integrity manifest in that word, and how by seeing an image of success on the inside of ourselves we can help ourselves progress in life in a more prosperous way. Sometimes though, our requests seem to fall on what people call, deaf ears as the saying goes, but I assure you they don't and the people that preach and teach that, the heavens are like brass to us, are not speaking scripturally correct. We have seen already that in **first John chapter five,** he states that;

> **14. "And this is the confidence that we have in him, that if we ask anything according to his will, he hears us."**

So that cancels that doctrine out straight away doesn't it? The Bible doesn't teach that God doesn't hear, but rather that He does, or that he ignores us because he doesn't. It does say that He resists the proud, but He still hears them.

No it's not that God's ears are deaf to us or that our requests are ignored. Sometimes it's a case of us not realizing that there are certain things that must happen for a reason. Now I'm not talking about getting healed, that's already done and you receive that the moment you ask as with everything else but healing has already come, you just have to receive it. We'll look at healing more specifically next.

What I'm talking about here are some of the other things that our lives involve, such as needs and circumstances like jobs and cars etc.

The principle I'm sharing here, is what some people call seed plant and harvest. You plant seed and then you harvest it for your crop. Well just as with seed you plant your seed and as the scripture pointed out you wait day and night, you sleep, you wait, you sleep, and eventually your seed sprouts up into what's called the blade. A lot of plants put up a first leaf that looks much like any other plants, however when the third leaf appears you can usually tell what kind of plant has germinated, but this involves waiting for a little bit and there in is the lesson, "The Standing".

Planting seed is good and then harvesting is good, the bit in the middle people think sometimes is not so good. It involves waiting sometimes. God has ordained that life on this planet evolves to some extent. I'm not talking about Evolution I'm saying God's way is to have things evolve over time, growth, progress; accomplishment often takes time because of the factors involved.

When we plant a seed we have to wait in the middle while the seed develops and grows into the plant full of fruit that it was destined and ordained by God to be. Just because the fruit is not on the plant the day after we planted the seed doesn't mean that your request has fallen on deaf ears or that your faith isn't working.

One of the fruits of the spirit of the re-born man is patience. This gift from God enables us to wait and be consistently the same in all circumstances, knowing that our faith is out there working as it should and it also enables us to wait assured that our seed is growing in the soil that God ordained should grow it.

Often I'm sure we've all prayed for things other than the things that have been specifically bought for us on the cross such as healing, which already belongs to us and we can receive and have manifest if we have faith. Other things though involve situations or other people at times, and these things follow God's laws of progression and produce after themselves.

(That simply means if you sow corn you get corn not carrots. If you sow bad things in life that's what you'll reap but sow love, and love will come back to you. Jesus spoke of casting your bread on the waters and in time it will come back on every wave. Which is why your giving produces more in the end, than you can use, and your prosperity overflows and takes over you the Bible says, (as an armed man). This law of Genesis says that if you sow in faith, you reap in faith, sow doubt, and you'll reap things of doubt. Hebrews tells us that;

> 12. "That you be not slothful, but followers of them who through faith and patience inherit the promises."
>
> 13. "For when God made promise to Abraham, because he could swear by no greater, he swear by himself,"
>
> 14. "Saying, surely blessing I will bless thee, and multiplying I will multiply thee."
>
> 15. "And so, after he had patiently endured, he obtained the promise." (Heb. 6 v 12-15)

We can see here that there is a time when we need to be patient and allow God to work because that's what's happening. It's not just time where the things you've prayed about are slipping away. If you received them when you prayed, you shall surely have them, (**Mk. 11 v 23**), your having though, has need of your patience while God orchestrates the circumstances necessary to bring about that which you have asked of Him.

Again we see in James;

> 2. "My brethren count it all joy when ye fall into diverse temptations;"
>
> 3. "Knowing this, that the trying of your faith worketh patience."
>
> 4. "But let patience have her perfect work, that ye may be perfect and entire, wanting nothing." (Jas. 1 v 2-4)

Now don't get the idea as some have preached that God is the one testing your faith, he isn't, (**Jas. 1 v 13**) remember we've already looked at who your adversary is and it's not God. Notice here in these scriptures that there is reward in being patient. Abraham received the promise, we are assured of maturity in God or perfection as it's translated if we will allow patients to have her way. The reason is that if we will, as it says, patiently wait for it, we will be able to obtain the thing we want, because God can get the people or things involved, that need to be in place, arranged accordingly. What satan does is to try and get you to dig up that seed of faith by being impatient and saying something negative about the situation. When you do everything stops dead in its tracks, until you get back in faith about it. It's not always easy to stand in faith, in fact if we're standing in faith it's usually a bit of a stretch, that's what faith is for not for the easy times when everything is going well. Our carnal mind tells us somehow that if we worry things will not be so bad, or that things will happen faster, or even that people will be more sympathetic toward us.

The problem with worry though, is that it makes us consider other options to faith and God's Word, and then we come unstuck. God is telling us here that patience is there for us to develop faith in, so as to be able to withstand the pressures associated with standing.

So many times I know, and have been told by God of others, that they were so close to receiving the requests they had brought to God, but had let go of their faith at the last minute, simply because they thought their prayers weren't getting answered, because it had been awhile. They thought that God had not given, or granted their request, because of the time factor involved. They see people born again, others receive their healing, and still others baptized in the Holy Ghost, only to feel that they have missed out. As I said some things that were bought at the cross by Jesus' sacrifice can be manifest in the natural instantly, but others need time to come to pass. If you pray for a new car and someone doesn't walk up to you in church on Sunday and say God told me to give you this car, they feel that their prayer has gone unanswered. It may sound silly but I'm just trying to help you see that although some things take time, it doesn't mean there not on the way. One preacher testified that God gave him a vision of a warehouse filled with things such as cars, arms, legs, new eyes, houses and lots more. When he asked God what were all these things, he was told that they are all the things and healings that people missed out on because they gave upon their faith to receive them. They had let satan talk or pressure them out of their blessings.

In the book of Ephesians were told that we wrestle against principalities and powers, rulers of the darkness of this world, **(Eph. 6 v 12)** the darkness is the ignorance of this world, the things that God's people are destroyed because of, and satan takes advantage of weakness and ignorance to deceive people. Jesus said that He is the light of the world and that we are also the light of the world. We don't and shouldn't allow evil forces to overcome our faith because Jesus already defeated them and gave us the authority and they know it. We're encouraged to put on the whole armour of God in verse eleven;

> **11. "Put on the whole armor of God that ye may be able to stand against the wiles of the devil."**

> **13. "In verse thirteen we are told to put this armor on so as we can stand in the evil day....."**

In verses fourteen to eighteen we're told exactly what that armor is:

14. "Stand therefore, having your loins girt about with truth, and having on the breastplate of righteousness;"

15. "And your feet shod with the preparation of the gospel of peace;"

16. "Above all taking the shield of faith, wherewith ye shall be able to quench all the fiery darts of the wicked."

17. "And take the helmet of salvation and the sword of the Spirit, which is the word of God:"

!8. "Praying always with all prayer and supplication in the Spirit and watching thereunto with all perseverance and supplication for all the saints."

Notice in the **thirteenth verse** we are told to put the armor on, then in the **fourteenth to the eighteenth verses** we are told what the armour is, but something that goes unnoticed by a lot of people and here again is an example of what we're talking about. At the end of **verse thirteen** and the beginning of **verse fourteen** it says that;

Having done all to stand, (that means put on the armor, pray the prayers, make your confession of faith, believe the Word of God and then, having done all to stand, "**STAND**". It sounds silly, and it looks too simple, but that's where a lot of people miss it with God. They simply fail (having done all they are instructed by God to do to stand) is to actually stand. The armor of God that He gives us to use is all designed to equip you to do just that, "to stand". Another way of saying to stand is to patiently wait in faith trusting in God to deliver, that which you have asked for, based on his promises in the Word.

In the Gospel of Luke Jesus says:

19. "In your patience posses your souls." (Lk. 21 v 20)

The Amplified Bible interprets this scripture to say;

19. "By your steadfastness and patient endurance you shall win the true life of your souls."

There is benefit and reward for the person that knows how to posses their soul in patience. Steadfastly waiting for God to manifest in your life that which he has promised. Possessing your soul means that it is anchored in the promise, so that you're not all over the place in doubt and wondering. Your soul (or your mind) is still, and at peace with the knowledge that you have what you've asked for.

As the parable of the sower tells us in the **eighth chapter and the fifteenth verse:**

15. "But that on the good ground are they, which in an honest and good heart, having heard the word keep it, and bring forth fruit with patience."

Notice here Jesus said those that keep the word, take it in their heart, believe it, say it out into the universe, live it, and keep it, will bring forth fruit with patience. Not just, will bring forth fruit, but will bring it forth with patience. It will take patience to bring some things to pass.

Do you remember earlier I told the story of my son's eye turning in? Well I had the answer the moment I asked for it, but it took time to come to pass. I asked God for a car I needed once and it seemed to some, that it was not coming, but each day I thanked God for my car. I said Lord you know I believe I have it, satan can't stop it coming, I know you've given it to me, so all I can think of is that someone's not doing their part. The next day a lady came to my house and said that God had told her to buy the car for me but that she had taken her time doing it, and asked me to forgive her. I did of course and we all benefited from the experience. I could have said "Oh! It's not coming", and let go of my faith, and the lady I'm sure, would have never gotten around to it. Faith with patience was the key to my success here. Faith with patience, gave God opportunity to arrange for the thing I'd asked for, to happen.

On some occasions patience is required more than at other times, particularly where money is required. God has to arrange for the person or persons who He has asked to give it to you, or who will make it available to you through work to become aware, and then to comply with God on the matter. If the person declines to give, which is his right, God will need to go to someone else with the opportunity to sow and reap before he can get you the money, and sometimes this takes time. God is telling me here there's something about giving he wants me to show you. It's off our subject slightly but God wants me to go into this for you here so I will. In **second Corinthians** we read;

> **6. "But this I say, He which soweth sparingly shall reap also sparingly; and He which soweth bountifully shall reap also bountifully."**
>
> **7. "Every man according as he purposeth in his heart, so let him give; not grudgingly or of necessity: for God loves a cheerful giver."**
>
> **8. "And God is able to make all grace abound toward you; that ye, always having all sufficiency n all things, may abound to every good work:"**

Notice here in verse seven that your giving is not of necessity. I don't know how many times I've heard preachers say that "your giving reflects your level of love or commitment etc. to God"; and just emotionally blackmail people into giving. Another comment I hear is that "God will tell you how much to give". That's like the statement that, God will pick your wife or husband for you. No! He doesn't want the responsibility of picking your partner or making your marriage work that's your job. If God picked someone then he would be responsible for everything in it. It's the same with your giving, it doesn't matter what anybody else says about it, if it doesn't line up with scripture it's rubbish, it's manipulative and it's worse than that, it's a lie and God will not bless it.

Verse six tells us the rule, the law or the principle that God is going to work on in these verses. The rule of, how you sow determines how you reap. Verse seven explains how the rule will be implemented, according as he purpose in his own heart, not grudgingly or of necessity and verse eight gives us the promise of what we can expect to happen, when we follow this to its conclusion, in regard to our giving.

Too often people are deceived and manipulated into giving by unscrupulous people, who are willing to misinterpret the scriptures to get you to give more. So read these scriptures, meditate them out and you will see what God is saying to us here about our giving. You see giving is a privilege, it brings a return just as sowing seed in the ground, that's why God relates sowing money to sowing seed both yield a return. Some people with a false humility will say "oh! I don't want or expect any return on my giving" they think it's humble to have martyrish attitudes about their giving. Well God wants us to receive on our giving. In Deuteronomy we're encouraged to tithe the Tithe by saying to God to "look down and bless us because of our giving" **(Deut. 26 v 13-15)**. Jesus taught us that sowing brings thirty sixty and a hundred fold return on our giving **(Matt. 13 v 8)(Mk. 10 v 30)**. As I said giving is a privilege not a necessity and God doesn't love you any less if you choose not to give, but why would you when the returns are so good? The reason God does anything is so that all may benefit from it, that's just the way He is, and getting when you give means more for you to use to help others. Anyway Like I said, all that was of the track a bit but now you're better informed as to God's will and that's what this book is for. It's God's will to also do it for you in the area of your finances amen?

> **1. "Wherefore seeing we are compassed about with so great a cloud of witnesses, let us lay aside every weight, and the sin which doth so easily beset us, and run with patience the race that is set before us."**

Here God tells us that this race we are in, and it must be a race or He would not have said it was, is supposed to be run with patience. We can try to run it with smarts, with cleverness or in some other way that we think our Christian lives should be run, but here God tells us to, run it with patience. We're told to fight the good fight of faith by Timothy **(1Tim. 6 v 12)** the reason it's called a good fight is because it's one that we win by being steadfast and proceeding with the force of patience until the end, and our fight is over and our race is run, and won. God will make sure we're successful. **God's will is to do it for you.**

I guess one of the most important things in life to most people is their health. It's something that can affect every part of our lives when it is not up to scratch.

When we are sick or dying there's little we can or feel like doing and it's a way the demons have of making us ineffective and ruining our testimony and robbing us of the life that God intended for us to have eternally, if we allow them get away with it. So let's look at healing more closely now we have learned about using our faith and trusting the integrity of God's Word, while being led by the Spirit.

Chapter Twelve

Healing
God Wants You Well

> **20. "He sent his Word, and healed them, and delivered them from their destructions."**
>
> **21. "Oh that men would praise the Lord for His goodness and for His wonderful works to the children of men."**

GOD SENT HIS Word the Bible says, and healed them. God's will is to do it for you. Notice it doesn't say that **It** healed them, meaning us the people, it says, **and** healed them. That's because God's word is not an it. He's a person, God and His Word are one. We are told in John's Gospel that the Word became flesh and dwelt among us:

> **14. "And the Word was made flesh, and dwelt among us, and we beheld his glory, the glory as of the only begotten of the Father, full of grace and truth." (Jn. 1 v 14)**

Jesus was the manifestation, amongst other things, of the healing power and the will of God to heal on the earth. A great many people believe that God does not heal today as He did in the time of Christ and the Apostles. Still others believe that God heals, but only under certain circumstances, most of which involve some form of elaborate ritual, and still others believe as I mentioned in the beginning, that God heals but He wouldn't heal them because they have not done anything worthy of being healed. Lastly there are those who believe God heals, and would heal them, but they just don't have the faith enough to receive. Instead of studying it out and building faith they just keep hoping someone with a gift will turn up to pray for them. The rest of the people just get healed, thank God, and go on.

In this chapter we'll build faith for healing and clear up some wrong thinking and if you need to be you will be closer to your own healing or to being able to help someone else to receive their healing. I can make that statement because healing has already come. Jesus already paid for it. The devil, the cause of all trouble has been defeated. Healing belongs to us based on God's word, according to the blessing which you became entitled to at The New Birth.

People might say well how can you say healing has already come when I'm still sick and didn't get it yet? That's just it, you didn't get it yet, but that's a different thing entirely to it hasn't come. The Bible says my people are destroyed through lack of knowledge **(Hos. 4 v 6)** just like everything else the devil gets away with it's just a matter of knowing the truth and believing God to give it to you.

I found that people are still confused about healings and where the lines are to be drawn. For instance there is Divine Healing, Divine Health and Divine Life. There is receiving by standing in faith and there is healing at the Altar when the Holy Spirit is ministering as a result of the corporate anointing of the service in progress. There are Gifts of Healings that operate in an Evangelist ministry for example this may sound a little confusing or too complicated but it's no different than opening the correct draw to get a knife and fork. You don't open every cupboard and draw in the house you simply go to where you know the cutlery is. That's the good thing about God's Word it clears up all the man made religious thinking that has stopped people receiving from God in the first place. God did everything that He did so we could have a better life, but we've confused it by making it harder with rules designed to exclude some.

Charles Capps a farmer, God called to preach and teach faith is credited with saying that the Bible is so simple to understand, that we've had to have help to misunderstand it. The concept that God is loving, caring and wants us to receive our healing that he's already provided, is almost impossible for some people to get their heads around. They have heard and been taught for so long that God is their

Judge and is vengeful that they couldn't imagine that He would do something nice for them, or cares enough to take any personal notice of them. So consequently, they can't believe He has already healed them and that healing is there for them to receive, just as electricity is at the plug for people to plug into and receive. The electricity has already come to the house and healing is right there in the spirit world, waiting for you to receive it with your faith.

If I were to say to you that there is electricity channeled to every home but it's only for those that have paid to receive it, you would say "oh! Ok, so we'll pay for electricity and then we can run our T.V.s and Toasters etc," but if I were to say to you however that you've paid but that you can't have any because the electric company doesn't think you deserve any, you would say, "What's that got to do with anything and what right do they have to disallow me?" And you'd be right to complain. You wouldn't think twice about fighting and believing for what is rightfully yours under our laws. However when it comes to healing people are disallowed by others on the basis of their opinion as to whether they deserve or not, based on church beliefs. The fact of the matter is, Jesus paid for your healing and God accepted that payment, and said that everybody, all people of every creed, race, religion, skin colour and any other thing you can think of are eligible if they will believe. Your electricity of healing is paid for, you qualify for a plug if you are a believer, your healing is at the plug, just plug in, stand in faith and turn it on, use what God has provided through Jesus.

In Matthew's Gospel we read;

> **23. "And Jesus went about all Galilee, teaching in their synagogues, and preaching the Gospel of the Kingdom, and healing all manner of sickness and all manner of diseases among the people." (Matt. 4 v 23)**

In the Gospel of Luke we see that Jesus said:

> **18. "The Spirit of the Lord is upon me because he has anointed me to preach the gospel to the poor; he has sent me to heal the broken**

hearted, to preach deliverance to the captives and to set at liberty them that are bruised,"

19. "To preach the acceptable year of the Lord." (Lk. 4 v 18)

We see here that Jesus went about healing all sickness and all diseases and said, "the Spirit of the Lord is on Him to…" to what? To do the things that the scriptures tell us, so if the Spirit of God was on Him to do those things, then they must be His will, in other words all these things are what God wants to happen for us. Matthew tells us;

14. "And when Jesus was come to Peters house he saw his wife's mother laid and sick of a fever."

15. "And he touched her hand and the fever left her and she arose and ministered to them."

16. "When the even was come they brought unto him many that were possessed with devils: and he cast out the spirits with his word and healed all that were sick."

17. "That it might be fulfilled which was spoken by Esaias the prophet saying, Himself took our infirmities and bare our sicknesses." (Matt. 8 v 14-17)

In this situation Jesus came across some one that was sick, and so He healed them. This is an example of Divine Healing. Most everybody in Christ has thought about the concept of being healed when they got sick. It's wonderful to be able to be made well when we feel so horrible, and are under attack from the enemy, and make no mistake, that's where your trouble comes from. We saw in an earlier chapter that God is not your problem He doesn't use sickness to teach us. He set Jesus' whole ministry against sickness and disease. The more convinced you are that sickness, disease, lack, confusion in fact any of the things under the curse is not God's will for you, the easier it will be to believe it has to go. It comes from satan but he's not your god anymore if you've accepted Jesus as your saviour. So don't take his gifts.

I was under attack one day with some kind of horrible flu thing from the pit of hell. I was thanking God for my healing and claiming my health, when the Spirit of God said to me "Son it's great that you believe me for your healing, but why do you wait until you're sick and then get healed, why don't you just stay well in the first place?" I was a bit taken aback and began to allow my mind to run over everything I could think of about healing, to see where this question could be answered. I love it when God asks a question because you know you've already seen the answer somewhere, and you're obviously missing it.

In the book of James we have two different examples of healing provision;

> **14. "Is any sick among you? Let him call for the Elders of the church; and let them pray over him anointing him with oil in the name of the Lord:"**
>
> **15. "And the prayer of faith shall save the sick, and the Lord shall raise him up; and if he have committed any sins they shall be forgiven him." (Jas. 5 v 14-15)**

Here is the promise to the immature Christian, who, when sick is in need of assistance to appropriate his healing. The oil is the point of contact for your faith and the symbol of the presence of the Holy Ghost. However, to be healed means you will have to get sick in the first place and since this is not in God's blessing for you, you don't have to be ill. I believe the secret lies in what the Holy Spirit showed me at the time of God's question to me. He said "Son you're not the sick trying to get healed, you are the well and the devil is trying to steal your health. You're already well, you have health I made you to be healthy and live an unlimited life". The devil has got people convinced that they must die, and most people believe they have to die sick. Now don't close the book, I know we all leave this planet, but you (your spirit person) don't die only your body does, you just change addresses. If you're saved you go to heaven **(2Cor5v6)** if not, the devil gets you at his place for an eternity, but you're not dead, and in fact you're more alive there than you are here. When I say, this was the promise for the immature Christian I'm talking about the person who is not mature in the Word, or at standing in faith. That doesn't mean you don't love God or haven't been saved for a number of years, because a lot of people who struggle with healing have been in Christ for years, but here again were talking about destruction through lack of knowledge. A lot of Christians, again because of their teaching, take on the fatalistic attitude and say, "If God wants to heal me He will." God has already healed us, we must take it by faith the same as our salvation, it must be a conscious step of faith to receive.

For the more mature Christian, those that have developed their faith in the work of the cross, in relation to healing, the Bible tells us this;

7. "Submit yourselves therefore to God, resist the devil and he will flee from you." (Jas. 4v7)

We are told here to resist the devil and he will flee. Well, he will have to because God said he would. He has no choice in the matter because Jesus defeated him in hell, and stripped him of any authority that Adam had given him. He must leave when you tell him to, believe it. What he does, is try to talk you out of it as we've already seen in the enemy chapter. So how do we resist the devil, do we call him names? No he just takes that as praise, unless you call him defeated and under the foot of the body of Christ, that upsets him. No we resist him the way Jesus did, we do it with the Word of God.

Notice here that God, through James, doesn't tell us to pray, he says resist him and he will go. Well if he goes the diseases and sicknesses go also, because he's the author of those things, him and his demon followers. God created life and health and satan has simply perverted what God created because he can't create anything of his own. It takes faith to create something and he doesn't have any. That's what the word evil means, a perversion of original truth and that's all he has ever done, is pervert any and everything he's ever come in contact with.

What the mature Christian is advised to do here is when a devil turns up in any form of sickness, is to say, "No! I don't receive that illness, I am the well not the sick and I refuse to agree with you that I am sick Jesus took that on the cross." Remember Jesus said if you agree as touching anything on earth it will come to pass. Don't use your authority to help the devil. Without your co-operation he's powerless to hurt you.

There are scriptures in the Bible that people think are contradictory and so have trouble believing against something they think may be from God. Here are a couple of these scriptures;

> **26. "And said, if you will diligently hearken to the voice of the Lord thy God and wilt do that which is right in his sight and wilt give ear to his commandments and keep all his statutes, I will put none of these diseases upon thee, which I have brought upon the Egyptians: for I am the Lord that healeth thee." (Ex. 15v26)**

> **27. "The Lord will smite thee with the botch of Egypt and with emerods and with the scab and with the itch whereof thou canst not be healed." (Deut. 28v27)**

The problem here is that the translators of the Old Testament from the Hebrew, didn't realize that there was a permissive and a causative verb in their language, and so the translation looks as though God said "I'll do it to you" when it should read, "That because of the position you're in or that you have adopted or taken I have no choice but to allow these things to come upon you". You see the curse was already in the earth but God was continually trying to save the people from the things under it. So when you read as in Hebrews;

Jesus Christ or the Word of God which He was manifest in the earth the same yesterday and today and forever **(Heb. 12v8)** you can be sure that He is. The apparent contradiction worries people because they think if He's good now how could He be cruel to people then, and if He was mean then, how could He be kind and loving now?

Well He couldn't, He said "You don't get bitter and sweet water from the same fountain" **(Jas. 3 v 11)** so the same is true with people and God. If that then is the case, God was both harsh then and now, or He was kind then and kind now.

If you look at the mistake in the translation, the life of Christ and the Love He showed us at the cross and the fact that the people in the Old Testament knew nothing of the evil one, you can see that God was good then and is good now, the same yesterday and today and healing is for us, and it was His idea that we should have it.

The Divine Life is what we will live when these mortal bodies of ours take on immortality. We at the New Birth received the life of God in our spirit man but we carry it around in an earthen vessel, or a body made from the ground.

> **6. "For God who commanded the light to shine out of darkness has shined in our hearts to give the light of the knowledge of the Glory of God in the face of Jesus Christ."**
>
> **7. "But we have this treasure in earthen vessels, that the excellency of the power maybe of God and not of us." (2Cor. 4 v 6-7)**

This divine life this glory of God that makes Him God that raised Jesus from the dead is inside us and is what caused us to re-born by the Spirit of God. With this in mind next time sickness or diseases come your way, say "no thanks God's in here and that stuff is just not appropriate."

When God created Man, the Earth and everything in it He gave dominion to His Man;

> **26. "And God said, Let us make man in our image after our likeness; And let them have dominion over the fish of the sea over the fowl of the air and over the cattle and over all the earth and over every creeping thing that creepeth on the earth." (Gen. 1v26)**

Mankind is the Jewel in the crown of God's creation, our authority at the time of creation stretched from Hell up to Heaven. Since Jesus redeemed us from the curse of the law our authority now stretches from within the gates of Hell, where satan can't hide from us anymore, right up to the very Throne of God. It is a tragedy that mankind having been given so much power and authority in Jesus name, still allows the devil to make us sick. The thing that has become the most dangerous to humans should be the least of our worries.

We know that man is the highest life form, then comes animals, birds, fish, all manner of creatures and bugs, plants, fungi, things like one celled creatures in the water and so on until we get right down to the bottom of this list where we get into much lower life forms such as a virus. We have the most dangerous viruses ever imagined in the world today, some of them we created ourselves under the inspiration of the devil. The fact is they are viruses not human beings with dominion from God. The devil has managed to convince us that the lower life forms have dominion over us, just as he convinced Eve that she could have something that she already had, if she would disobey God's word. These so called killer viruses that some are so afraid of, are only so, because we are convinced that they are powerful, to the extent that they could kill anybody anytime.

John G Laker went to Africa to work with victims of the plague, but he didn't get sick like everyone else.

When they asked him why he said to them to take a Petri dish with the virus growing in it and place it in his hand. He then asked them to examine the dish again under the microscope and tell him what they saw.

When the people looked at the dish they saw that the virus was dead. He told them that the righteousness of God killed it. This man knew who he was in Christ he knew these things do not have dominion over us the people with the life of God on the inside. In historical America Abraham Lincoln freed the slaves. He said that men should be free, but it was a long time before people put any faith in that and stood their ground based on the law, but when they did it protected them. You see a law is useless unless you put it to the test and watch it justify the situation. Similarly the Law of the Spirit of Life in Christ Jesus that has made us free from the law of sin and death **(Rom 8v2)** is no good to us until we put some faith in it.

Many years ago I used to suffer from migraine headaches. The first time I had one, was when I was about twelve years old. I was riding my bike back from a swimming pool with a friend. The pain in my head was so bad I had to stop and lay down on the footpath alongside a main road my friend stopped a car and the driver took me home. I remember the pain to this day and everyone I had after that. If you've ever had one you know what I'm talking about, it's the most intense blinding pain, that just doesn't let up for hours, and it leaves you drained for days.

Well I suffered with these headaches for years, until I began to mature in my attitude and understanding of the Word and its application in faith. There came a time when I was attacked with a migraine again but this time I said no to it. I lay on my bed and took authority over this thing in the name of Jesus. I took no medication, I just simply said no I'm the well I'm healed and delivered from these migraine headaches and thanked the Lord for my healing. Now when I began the head ache still took a while to go and the devil was at my mind with, "see it's not working, just take the pills," but I knew, that if I was to beat this thing God's Word had to be enough. I knew I would be delivered if I stood my ground. Well like I said, eventually it went and I was happy to give God the thanks for my relief.

The next time I was attacked with a headache, I did the same thing, but this time it went a lot quicker and I felt in myself that I was healed and delivered at last of this demonic oppression. A few years later after teaching at a youth camp for the week end, I returned home, and while telling my wife about the wonderful things God was able to do in the lives of those young people, I was suddenly attacked with a vicious migraine. I knew in my spirit that the devil was trying to punish me for my work and trying to get me to receive those headaches back in my life. I lay down for a short while and said, "No I'm done with this stuff, I'm healed, and I got up and had my tea, and I have never had another since. That was all of eighteen years ago and I still thank God for the things such as this that He's delivered me from. It's great when your faith works and you see the Holy Spirit working in your life. Jesus is alive hallelujah.

This then is an example of resisting the devil and watching him flee. Once you begin to chase him off for some of the small things, you are less afraid of bigger things, because he has no more power with them than with the small stuff.

Jesus is Lord of all. Interesting to notice something here too, and that is that, the three score and ten referred to in the Bible as mans length of days allotted to him to live is not necessarily relevant to us now under the New Covenant. In the book of Psalms we read;

> **10. "The days of our years are threescore years and ten; and if by strength they be fourscore years, yet is their strength labour and sorrow; for it is soon cut off, and we fly away." (Pslm. 90 v 10)**

This scripture is telling us we really only get seventy years and if we manage to live longer through strength and be proud of it we still only get a little more time to suffer at an old age. We're told in the book of Revelation that Jesus holds the keys of hell and death **(Rev 1v18)**. Well if Jesus holds the keys of hell and death and death was under the curse, that Jesus freed us from, then he freed us from death. If we're free from death then we don't have to do it, any more than anything else we've been delivered from. We just finish our time and work here and then go home to be with the Lord. There's a difference between going home and dying. Going home is an appointed activity in the Lord, where as dying is having our lives taken before our time and that was part of the curse.

The Bible tells us in Romans;

> **14. "For sin shall not have dominion over you: for ye are not under the law, but under grace." (Rom. 6 v 14)**

The reason mankind became subject to death was because of the fall of man, because the curse came into being due to Adams transgression in the garden. The transgression of God's Word brought the law and the law brought with it the penalty of death for sin. Jesus redeemed us from the curse of the law being made a curse for us, because it's written cursed is everyone that hangs on the tree, **(Gal. 3 v 13)** and so if He has redeemed us from the curse he has redeemed us from death, which was under the curse. If we are then redeemed from death there is no reason to accept anything that is likely to bring it on, such as sickness and disease etc. Can you see the logic in that? Now you might still be struggling with the fact that we don't have to die, but remember I said, we all pass on (it's appointed to everyman once to die and after that the judgment. **(Heb 9 v 27)** It's just that you don't have to go sick, and will no longer be judged for your sins, but rather for reward, if you are God's, you are passed from judgment unto life;

> **14. "We know that we have passed from death unto life, because we love the brethren. He that loveth not his brother abideth in death." (1Jn. 3 v 14)**

And again Paul tells us;

> **2. "For the law of the spirit of life in Christ Jesus hath made me free from the law of sin and death." (Rom. 8 v 2)**

We are set free from being subject to death and that is not just spiritual death Jesus died physically and spiritually when He was separated from the Father, else how could He have been our substitute and the price of our sin?

Hebrews tells us that;

> **14. "Forasmuch then as the children are partakers of flesh and blood, he also himself likewise took part of the same; that through death he might destroy him that had the power of death, that is, the devil." (Heb. 2 v 14)**

> **15. "And deliver them who through fear of death were all their life time subject to bondage." (Heb. 2 v 14-15)**

Jesus came and shared with us in that he came in the flesh and because of that, now allows us to share in the health and wellbeing that he enjoys, having defeated death and sickness for us. We see that just as with any other subject, that it's our belief in the power of death that gave death its power in the first place, (**Heb. 2 Verse 15**), having been told now by God that we are free from it we should have no more fear. If there is no more fear then death has no power to overcome us in any way. We are free until the Lord says it's our time. Just like anything else in God, we must hold on to that promise in faith. God wants you well He does not get any glory out of people being sick and dying. God doesn't give you death, where would he get it? The Bible says he is Life, Light, Righteousness, Love, Peace and Joy in the Holy Ghost; He's understanding, Wisdom, Gentleness, and Good. When Jesus was on the earth he said that he only did and said what he saw and heard of the Father. Not once does the Bible tell us anywhere, that Jesus was selfish, sick or insecure. If you've got trouble or sickness attacking you, it's not from God He doesn't have any, so stand against it.

There are people who actually hinder the work of the cross in regard to their own healing just as they did when Jesus walked the earth. In his time it was because of their unbelief and now people hinder the work of Christ in their life by their wrong belief as well. Some people are very dedicated to what they believe is the will of God they are sincere but sincerely wrong and their beliefs that healing has passed away or that we are to share in the sufferings of Christ. Believing that means sickness and disease, is wrong thinking, and is costing them their health and at times their lives.

I've heard people with my own ears say that, God is using a cold or some ache or pain to slow them down, so as to have them rest. In the first place why would God want you to slow down working for Him, when the harvest is so ripe? Working for God under the blessing would only make you healthier anyway not sicker, and secondly because as we've seen, God is a good God not a criminal.

If you had the power to make people sick and used it to do so, when you were found out, you would be prosecuted. It's from God's Word that all beneficial laws and legal protection are derived in the first place, so why would God use illegal methods to do His will and then like a hypocrite tell us to obey the laws of the land, and that the authorities are not placed there in vain? That would be a sin and God does not sin.

No! God does not use sickness or pain to teach us. The Bible tells us that we are taught by the use of the Word;

> 14. "But strong meat belongeth to them that are of full age, even those who by reason of use have their senses exercised to discern both good and evil." (Heb. 5 v 14)

Notice it does not say we are punished or hurt or scared into learning or obeying. It says that we are educated or that our senses are trained to discern between good and evil. God teaches us the differences between what's good for us and what isn't, like sickness, by using the Word to train us. Follow the Word and you'll follow after health. Stop and say this out loud right now, "I'm healthier right now than I've ever been, because Jesus bought my healing on the cross two thousand years ago. I am well in Jesus name." Say it every day and you'll live better. The Bible shows us the importance of saying good things;

> 20. "A man's belly shall be satisfied by the fruit of his mouth; and with the increase of his lips shall he be filled."
>
> 21. "Death and life are in the power of the tongue: and they that love it shall eat the fruit thereof." (Prov. 18 v 20-21)
>
> 2. "Bless the Lord O my soul, and forget not all his benefits:"
>
> 3. "Who forgiveth all thine iniquities; who healeth all thine diseases;"
>
> 4. "Who redeemeth thy life from destruction; who crowneth thee with loving kindness and tender mercies."

> **5. "Who satisfieth thy mouth with good things, so that thy youth is renewed like the eagles." (Prov. 103 v 2-5)**

Who satisfies our mouth so our youth is renewed. God has said that if we speak the good things He has provided we get renewed. Well what good things has he given to us? Well remember in Peter he said that He's given us, all things that pertain to life and Godliness through the knowledge of Jesus the Word of God **(2Pet. 1 v 3)** and so he is saying, we will be renewed by speaking out the Word. To be renewed is to be made young again and what are people generally when they are younger? They are healthier brighter and stronger. Notice also we just read that Life and Death are in the power of the tongue and we will eat which ever fruit we choose to talk. Speaking words of faith and wellness will keep you well.

> **23. "The heart of the wise teacheth his mouth, and addeth learning to his lips."**
>
> **24. "Pleasant words are as a honeycomb, sweet to the soul, and health to the bones." (Prov. 16 v 23-24)**

And again we see;

> **3. "He that keepeth his mouth keepeth his life: but he that openeth wide his lips shall have destruction." (Prov. 13 v 3)**

The word of God is full of teaching about watching what we say in relation to our healing and staying healthy. We think we are being honest to say were sick but we're just making it worse by giving it power.

Some old songs etc. say that "God's going to get you for that" and so on. If God wanted to get you you'd be got already, after all It's pretty hard to hide from a guy that's all powerful and omnipresent (everywhere). No God's desire for us is that we are healthy in every area of our lives, spiritually strong, moving in faith, and in the gifts of the Holy Spirit, able to withstand the pressures of the unseen world and mature in the Word, mentally well adjusted having the mind of Christ, aligning our will with His, having our minds renewed and being transformed into the likeness of Christ more and more every day; being physically healthy in our mortal bodies, living victorious, and walking in the newness of life. Not being subject to the symptoms and illnesses that afflict the world today. Having a walking talking testimony of power over sickness and disease in the Name of Jesus Christ of Nazareth, Hallelujah! Once you are living the victorious life Jesus intended for us, you can teach others how to do the same and they in turn will do that, making the devils life a misery instead of the other way round.

A friend of ours has a small child that was afflicted with a foul virus or some such thing the other week and had taken her into the hospital for a couple of days. She told us that her child was struggling and didn't seem to be improving. I thought about the poor little saint for a moment and God told me to get a handkerchief and pray over it and place it on the child. Well as my wife was about to go and see the infant, I told her what the Lord had said and gave her the cloth to take in. The testimony of the mother later was that within a half an hour of the hanky going on the child she was up and running about. God has also since delivered her from asthma attacks. God is good and will always honor your faith after all, it is God's will that you are well.

I've spoken to ministers that are just too afraid to promise or say come out for prayer because God has healed you. They say what if it doesn't work the person will be very disillusioned? These people I'm sorry to say are simply more interested in their reputation or their position than in the ministration of the Word and the Love of God, and sadly lacking in confidence in their God's ability and willingness to meet the needs of the people. Jesus healed all that came to Him, some immediately, some within the hour and so on. If you are going to represent the Master you should at least be willing to give a true representation of what he has promised. For centuries people have been watering down the Gospel promises because they are embarrassed that God won't move. The thing we need to understand is that healing always comes it's just not always received, I mentioned this sort of thing earlier. It's not our job to see that healing comes to pass that's the job of the Holy Spirit and He's good at it. All we are asked to do is to present the truth and allow people to act on it and by praying for the sick, dying, aids infected, crippled and oppressed etc. we give them the chance to believe God and receive their healing. It's not our responsibility to bring it to pass, so people should stop worrying about what will or won't work and take God at His word and pray believing.

Unbelief or wrong believing is a real hindrance to receiving from God. Some other hindrances are not being prepared to receive. If you are going to go to God about your healing make sure you are prepared to receive. Make sure you understand what you need. Meditate on the healing scriptures so as your heart and mind is full of the faith and confidence that healing will come, and that it's for you right now. Be assured that it is God's will to heal, you can't afford to doubt, and make sure you have no root of bitterness, because this will hinder the work of the Holy Spirit;

> **30. "And grieve not the Holy Spirit, whereby ye are sealed unto the day of redemption."**
>
> **31. "Let all bitterness, and wrath and anger, and clamor, and evil speaking, be put away from you, with all malice:**
>
> **32. "And be ye kind one to another, tenderhearted, forgiving one another, even as God for Christ's sake hath forgiven you." (Eph. 4 v 30-32)**

Notice here that Paul tells us that bitterness etc. grieves the Holy Spirit, and if you're grieving the Spirit of God you are out of love. Not walking in love will hinder your healing, because you will not be confident toward God in your faith to receive.

Forsake hero worship. I mentioned earlier in the book about the lady who came forward for prayer in relation to cancer. When I asked her what she wanted from me she answered "to heal me from cancer" so I told her to sit down I couldn't help her. On returning to the Altar a few moments later she said "I get it, I want Jesus to heal me".

40. "He that receiveth you receiveth me, and he that receiveth me receiveth him that sent me." (Matt. 10 v 40)

Jesus tells us here in Matthew's Gospel that if someone is receiving us in some capacity, whether it be as the one who administers healing or counselling or teaching, in receiving us or what we are offering at the time, they are really receiving Jesus, because he is the word and if they receive Jesus then God, who is the author of all life. So it may come through a man by faith in the word, but it is coming from God not any other person, so always look to God as your healer and source not a man, no matter how famous he might be.

2. "Looking unto Jesus the author and finisher of our faith; who for the joy that was set before him endured the cross, despising the shame, and is set down at the right hand of the throne of God."

3. "For consider him that endured such contradiction of sinners against himself, lest ye be wearied and faint in your minds." (Heb 12 v 2-3)

The Bible here tells us to consider Jesus the author and finisher of our faith. Notice it doesn't say consider the sickness, or to consider our own capacity to deal with our illnesses, (and they're not our illnesses anyway they belong to the devil) and he can keep them, no it says consider Jesus. It also doesn't tell us to consider what happened to anyone else that stood against the same thing either.

You really don't know what was in their heart if they didn't receive their healing. Their success or failure either way is not the criteria for you to receive or not. What is relevant is what Jesus did on the cross, and your faith in it.

Well how do we consider Jesus? We think about what He has done, meditate the price He has paid for our redemption and how he suffered for us, then we take communion in thanks and tell the sickness to get away from us.

The sufferings spoken about in the Bible that we share with Christ do not refer to sickness, but to rejections and persecution by those who don't or won't understand the love of God in us. There are many words and statements in the Bible that we have taken the wrong way and led people to believe that God was their problem, or that we simply have to have some of these things that Christ actually died to free us from, like the word afflictions. The Bible says that many are the afflictions of the righteous. **(Pslm. 34 v 19)** and again in **(Col. 1 v 24)** we see the words afflictions and sufferings both refer to trouble and persecutions. While trouble and persecutions are not something to be received with gladness either, they are not sickness, so again we can be confident that when the bible tells us that persecution will come for some reason, it is not referring to sickness or disease. Again the more convinced we are that God wants us well, the more likely we will be to stand against it in Jesus name, and if you stand in faith you will win.

> **29. "Let no corrupt communication proceed out of your mouth, but that which is good to the use of edifying, that it may minister grace to the hearers." (Eph. 4v29)**

We are warned here of the dangers of corrupt communication, which is evil communication with evil meaning, a perversion or changing of an original truth. To say that God puts sickness on people is a fairly obvious statement for most Christians to see through, but something that appears to be a little more subtle and catches people out is making the corrupt statement that "I am sick." Now a lot of people wouldn't consider that to be an evil statement, even if they thought that it's not good for their health to agree with it. But that's exactly what it is, an evil statement. Its evil conversation in that, the Bible says in (**1Peter 2 v 24**) that by His stripes you were past tense healed.

To say you are sick as a born again Christian, is to make two corrupt statements firstly to call God a liar, because He said "you're healed" and to say you're sick, is just a complete perversion of the truth. Now God doesn't treat us as though that's what we're doing because He is compassionate and loving and knows that if we knew better people wouldn't say it, but the reality is, that's what people do if they say," I'm sick or broke or weak". God said, "Let the weak say

I am strong". Or if we say, "I can't do something" because the Bible tells us we can do all things etc. so you can see our confession is important on several levels if we are to stay well and strong or receive the healing needed. In the **twenty third Psalm** which begins;

1. "The Lord is my shepherd; I shall not want." (Pslm. 23 v 1)

This is the first two lines of the psalm, and in fact, is the whole Psalm in one respect, because everything that comes after it is simply examples of this first qualifying statement. The Psalmist goes on to say under the inspiration of the Holy Spirit, amongst other things that, God prepares a table for us in the presence of our enemies. A lot of people talk about having victory over our enemies, being rich, having no more sickness and so on when we go to heaven. Well this Psalm talks of having a table set before us in the presence of our enemies.

Our enemies won't be in heaven, there here with us right now, and so that's where the table set before us, in their presence, which is right here, right now. On that table are bowls filled with Prosperity, Healing, Redemption, Angels, the Blood of the Lamb, everything Jesus bought for us on the Cross at Calvary. This table is set here in front of the devil and all his cohorts and they have to watch us eat from it, our fill of Healing, Peace, Joy, and Love by faith and there's nothing they can do to stop you getting it all, accept to talk and beguile you out of your share, Just as they did Adam and Eve.

I think the greatest hindrance to receiving healing or anything else from God is our lack of righteousness consciousness, not our lack of righteousness, because Jesus has made us righteous, **(Rom 5 v 18)** but our lack of a righteousness consciousness. It's this consciousness that will produce the attitude that says, "You can't put that sickness on me I'm the body of Christ". If you're not convinced of your right standing with God you won't be able to confidently expect God to move for you as quickly as he would Jesus. We are told in the book of **Hebrews in the tenth chapter,** that in the Bible times the sacrifices the people made couldn't really cleanse them the way the Blood of Jesus has us, and so they had to keep making them because they were continually conscious of their sins before God. So what God is saying here to us is, that we should now have no more consciousness of our sin, now I didn't say we have no sin or that we don't sin, **(1Jn. 1 v9)** tells us that God is faithful to forgive when we sin so we do obviously, but we should feel when we come before God with our requests as though we have never sinned. That's how He sees us thanks to the blood, and therefore we should be confident of receiving our healing from God.

> **4. "Who gave himself for our sins, that he might deliver us from this present evil world, according to the will of God and our Father." (Gal. 1 v 4)**

> **26. "For ye are all the children of God by faith in Christ Jesus."**

> **29. "And if ye be Christ's, then are ye Abraham's seed, and heirs according to the promise." (Gal. 3 v 26+29)**

 Here we are assured of being God's children, and that is not possible unless you are cleansed of your sin, and that we are heirs joint heirs with the Christ. It is as if every scripture in the Bible is telling us that we are to receive, receive, and receive from God. Receive Righteousness, Prosperity, Love, Guidance, Comfort, Counsel, Provision, Teaching, Deliverance and certainly Healing. Many of us can accept that God would save us, but think He won't necessarily heal us.

 (I Peter 2 v24) Tells us that He bore our sins in his own body and by whose stripes we were healed. It's the same scripture why do people break it into two different things to consider? If He saved you, He has healed you.

 If you have the faith to believe you are saved, you have the faith to believe you're healed. The problem with this consideration comes from the fact that we really don't have the opposition evidence against our salvation the way we do in regard to healing. With healing we are attacked and have fears, pain, Doctors and the devil, all telling us we're sick, and we are pressured to consider those opinions and symptoms instead of Jesus as the Word tells us to. Jesus is the Word considering what the Word says about your situation instead of the sickness, is to be considering Jesus.

Further to this there are people in the Body of Christ that teach that these scriptures relate to spiritual healing only.

This is a false doctrine the word salvation comes from the Greek word Soteria, meaning total safety, and total deliverance, not just deliverance from sin, and not just healing or deliverance spiritually but not physically, it means total deliverance, spiritually, mentally, physically, financially and socially, that's the whole lot. He didn't leave anything out. So to split up scripture promises to justify something we haven't been able to acquire through a lack of faith, is to accuse God of partiality and false promises, and of being unjust, in that He promises things we can't access, and He doesn't. Don't split scripture into spiritual and carnal, or physical elements and hinder your own healing chances.

If spiritual healing was all Jesus bought for us at the cross, what was that beating He took for then? He could have just died, just slipped away and took care of business in hell. A roman Centurion who crucified people on a daily basis for a living, said of Jesus that, He looked so bad that God must have done this to Him, because no man could be beaten so badly without dying. Jesus took that beating and then the subsequent crucifixion and separation from God, which is spiritual death, to ensure that we were delivered both spiritually and physically. Again, God is not a respecter of persons, **(Act. 10 v 34)** and so if He's ever healed anybody, then He has healed you and me.

In the book of Romans Paul tell us that;

> **16. "For I am not ashamed of the Gospel of Christ: for it is the power of God unto salvation to everyone that believeth; to the Jew first, and also to the Greek."**
>
> **17. "For therein is the righteousness of God revealed from faith to faith: as it is written, the just shall live by faith." (Rom. 1 v 16-17)**

As you see, the Gospel is the power of God unto salvation or unto soteria to everyone that believes. If you are a believer, the Gospel that you believe, affords you on the authority of God himself, total deliverance from any sickness and disease that might present its self for your acceptance. "The just shall live by faith", having faith in the redemptive work of the cross in relation to healing, will cause you to be healed, live and not die sick.

When I first began standing for my healing, and by that I mean when I had made the decision that come what may I was not going to rely on the Doctors, or on taking medication ever again. Now that was my stand, everyone has to start where and in a way that they choose. I remember when people found out what I was doing they, as I've mentioned earlier, had mixed reactions, some were encouraging and some weren't but never the less I had decided and that was that. I did by the way take my own stand long before I expected my wife or children to believe God for their healing, and as I've already shared the Asthma attacks that came against my daughter were where I began trusting God and standing in faith for my children. Anyway I would be attacked with something and I would pray and believe God's Word that I was healed. It used to bother me though that I would get attacked when I knew satan was defeated. People would make remarks like "I thought you believed in healing" and were always quick to ask if I had a cold, should I show the slightest sign of a sniffle. Well bless their hearts they just got caught being silly, but I'm sure some of them these days have got the revelation on healing. I would as I said take my stand but it always bothered me that people would see I still got things I had to deal with. Later on I became stronger in my faith and the assurance that I am the well as I said, not the sick. The thing I want to encourage you with here is that when I spoke to God about it at that time he said to me "Son an attack is not a sign of failure." This is how people made me feel if they commented about my health not being perfect on any given day. They made me feel as though I was failing because of the symptoms I was showing, but when God said to me that it wasn't a sign of failure simply that I was getting attacked. He said "that as long as you're on this earth you'll be attacked, but you don't have to be defeated", an attack is not a sign of failure, it's just a sign that you are in a fight, and satan can't fight for long because he has no faith.

He or any other demon that he sends to trouble you in your life will want a quick victory, they can't afford to fail at their job or the devil will punish them. If it's the devil himself he doesn't want to look bad and weak in front of his cohorts so he won't keep up the fight indefinitely, he will leave for another time and opportunity, that's why the Bible tells us not to give him a foothold. If you don't give him a foothold he can't climb all over you. So don't let thoughts of failure enter your thinking and hinder you're receiving just because you're in a battle.

It's a form of fainting in your mind let's look again at the scripture in Hebrews where the Bible tells us;

> **3. "For consider him that endured such contradiction of sinners against himself, lest you be wearied and faint in your minds." (Heb. 12 v 3)**

Often when you're standing for your healing you feel sometimes that the problem is getting bigger and the devil stronger and you're losing the fight. That's not true. The devil comes to you with that rubbish to psych you out, he tells you you're losing and that you'd better try something else. The truth of the matter is that you're probably very close to your breakthrough and he knows it. You see if we let him psych us out we begin to feel weaker, but if we get back on the word, speak our faith, and stay with God through the whole thing, we will keep up our strength and you'll see that the devil isn't getting stronger, we were just fainting on the job, we were getting weary of the battle because our faith tank is running dry. Keep your faith level up and feed on the word day and night because, believe it or not, the devil hits you first up with his best shot. If you took that you can defeat him, because that's all he's got. You on the other hand can grow in faith every day and you have the Holy Spirit to help, the Blood of the Lamb working for you and the right standing or righteousness it affords you scares satan to death. He knows he's already been beaten, God knows it, the Holy Ghost, Jesus and all the Angels, they saw it, they saw and bore witness to the defeat satan suffered at the hand of the Lord, so stand your ground and stay in the word so as you don't faint in your mind.

Let's look at this scripture in Proverbs;

20. "My son, attend to my words;
incline thine ear to my saying."

21. "Let them not depart from thine eyes;
keep them in the midst of thine heart."

22. "For they are life unto those that find
them and health to all their flesh."

23. "Keep thy heart with all diligence;
for out of it are the issues of life."

24. "Put away from thee a forward mouth, and
perverse lips put far from thee." (Prov. 4v20-24)

These verses begin with the words my son, indicating God's attitude towards us as his children. He is saying to us here that I care about you as my dear children, as a loving father would. He could of said "I God tell you this", but He didn't, He wanted us to grasp the gravity of His caring, He wanted to impact on our thinking that He sees us as His responsibility, as dear children not just a bunch of people that He is Lording it over.

If you have someone who you love and that you know without a shadow of a doubt that they love you, you would trust them. If you also knew that they were fully able to do everything they said they could and would do for you, you would trust them implicitly. God wants us to realize from these and other scriptures that He has a great love and a desire to care for us as our parent. If you didn't have a loving father or care giver it may be harder for you to relate to God with a relaxed happy understanding of that concept automatically, so you will have to take His love and trust that He is a gentle and loving father, by faith. Give him the benefit and reap a reward for your trust. You have nothing to lose and everything to gain.

Secondly He says, attend to my words; the word attend here means to prick up your ears, focus on, make sure you pay close attention to what is being said with a view to clearly understanding what is meant and implied. That's the Robbie translated version.

Again God here is taking responsibility for our welfare by making sure we give attention so as not to miss what he is saying. "Attend" He says, "Hey look at me and listen, so you know what is going on here" and so on. I remember many time saying to my own children "Hey listen to me, I want you to do this or that or I don't want you to do this or that." What I was doing was to make sure they knew what I wanted, and that I knew they had got the message. I didn't want to have a problem with them, or for them to have a problem with something else later on. I wanted to make sure things were clear, so as they were safe and well. It wasn't about being right or bossing them around, it was about knowing more than they did about things and situations and making sure they were cared for in them and God is no different, He is a living spiritual parent, where do you think we got that level of responsibility from in the first place? The Bible says "What have you got that you did not receive?" The care and love in our own souls for our children comes from the inside of God. He is doing the same thing I used to do He is making sure we get it right.

He says, "My children attend to my words." It's His words that He knows will help us, because he knows all about the universe. Sometimes I make the statement to people that God is smarter than we are, and they look at me like I've just made the most obvious statement in the world. Well it probably is if you think about it, but we often don't obviously because so many people still try everything they can think of before coming to God with the problem. If saying God knows more than we do is such an obvious thing why don't people go to God first? It's that old saying from somewhere of years ago again, that someone was worrying and another said to them, "We could always pray", and they answered "Oh no! Has it come to that?"

We've looked at the integrity of God's word already and we know it can be trusted because He is faithful and He has the ability to perform it, but it is also, and again I'll state the obvious for effect, God's word is right, correct, the best option because He knows. It's so important to have this revelation if we are going to continually trust and receive from God without hindrance.

He goes on to say next that we should incline our ear unto just what it is that He is saying;

**27. "What I tell you in darkness, that speak
ye in light: and what ye hear in the ear, that
preach ye upon the house tops." (Matt. 10 v 27)**

God is showing us here, that the things He speaks to us are the important things worth shouting about, the things that we should be operating on in our own lives. Jesus himself warned the disciples and of course we ourselves indirectly, to take head what we hear;

**24. "Take head what ye hear: with what measure
ye mete, it shall be measured to you: and unto
you that hear more shall be given." (Mk. 4 v 24)**

Jesus is telling us to be careful what we hear, be careful what we let into our heads, the things we hear and give our attention to will ultimately determine the direction our thought life will be travelling and that will determine our life. The amount of attention and study we give to what we hear will come back to us good or bad. If it's God's word we are studying then it will give us more of what is good. More faith, more healing, more peace, more joy and so on. If it's not we run the risk of losing even that which we had as the next verse goes on to tell;

**25. "For he that has to him shall be given:
and he that has not, from him shall be taken
even that which he has." (Mk. 4 v 25)**

The warning here is that if we are not listening to the word but instead filling our ears with something else less productive and less protective then we run the risk of failure or worse. The scripture says that we lose even that which we have, we lose our faith health whatever but even more disturbing is that the implication is that it is taken away from us by force. I believe this is referring to the enemy who when we are not on the word is more than a match for us in our lives. He is defeated but it was the Word of God that beat him, we must always be in God's strength not our own.

There is a scripture that I'm particularly fond of I will share with you here in relation to having more given as we hear;

> **9.** "For this cause we also, since the day we heard it, do not cease to pray for you, and to desire that you might be filled with the knowledge of his will in all wisdom and spiritual understanding;"
>
> **10.** "That ye might walk worthy of the Lord unto all pleasing, being fruitful in every good work, increasing in the knowledge of God." (Col. 1 v 9-10)

Notice here Paul prays in verse nine that we would be filled with the Knowledge of God's will, then in **verse 10** he says he wants us to increase in the knowledge of God. Since God and his will and his word are all the same thing I began to wonder why the Apostle Paul would have said it twice because if you've been filled how then can you increase? If you are full you are full. I asked the Lord about it and He showed me this.

When God shows you something for the first time it's all new to us and we then have to put those things God has shown us into practice somehow. When this happens and we become experienced at operating in faith in that area, we grow, and because we grow in faith, in knowledge of operation and in relation to the subject God is dealing with us in; We then have a greater capacity for that subject, we can in fact then take in more in relation to that teaching. So we were full then we grew because of the revelation and therefore were able to handle a greater amount of the revelation, which in turn would cause us to grow again. You see when we incline our ear to the word of God we grow and the more we grow the less likely we are to lose that which we already have, and as another bonus these areas of growth are not just spiritual as we will see in a minute.

The scripture verse said to us to "incline our ear to". God is telling us here that He will give us the good word, and look after us as His children etc. But we have a responsibility in this as well and that is to do the inclining. That means a deliberate act of our will in obedience to the Word out of respect for God and his love. Just as my heart was for my children, and my desire was that they remain safe and healthy. If they took little or no notice of what I had said to them in that regard, the outcome of any given day might have been very different. So too with God, if we do not diligently listen to His Word we may live to regret it.

Verse 21 goes on to say **let them** (the sayings or his word) **not depart from thine eye**s;"

If our eyes are fixed on the word then we will not be looking at the problem. What has our focus has us. If we meditate on the Word looking at what it says, building faith for that subject, then we won't be looking at the worries of the particular trial. The devil will not be able to persecute us in our minds where the battle for this life is fort. He will not be able to make us faint or psych us out.

The writer goes on to say to keep them in the midst of thine heart and further along in **verse 23** he says **"keep your heart with all diligence for out of it are the issues of life."**

When the Bible speaks about our heart, it is not referring to the blood pump that keeps our blood circulating, nor is it talking about our emotions as in some old love story where we use phrases such as my heart longs for you etc. Here God is referring to your spirit man, your inner you, the real you, not this body, this vehicle that we travel around in, but the person of yourself, you. This is who God see's when the Bible tells us that God doesn't judge by the flesh, but sees the heart of a person. He is looking at the real you. You see we are spirit soul and body. We are a spirit being, we have a soul, (emotions, intellect and a will), and we live inside a body, (or this earth vehicle). When you leave this vehicle you leave this earth. Don't be fooled by Hollywood movies when you leave this body you leave this earth. You don't wander around this earth waiting for justice or the Ghost Whisperer to understand you; Any spirit being wandering around without a body, unless their Angels are demon spirits trying to express themselves through people or animals in some way.

Jesus tells us;

> **45. "A good man out of the good treasure of his heart bringeth forth that which is good; and an evil man out of the evil treasure of his heart bringeth forth that which is evil: for of the abundance of the heart the mouth speaketh." (Lk. 6 v 45)**

We are told to keep the Word in our heart and then to guard our heart with all diligence, to watch over it making very sure as to what goes into it. This is because the scripture tells us, that out of our heart or our spirit man flows, or come from, the issues of life. So what are the issues of life?

They are the issues or the forces that keep you alive, the forces that issue life to your body and soul, your mind. It's your spirit man that keeps your body alive, without the spirit being in your body it just reverts back to its original materials and state, the dirt of the earth. Your spirit was created by God from the very life within God himself. That's why a spirit being can't actually die in the sense we think of things dying. A spirit doesn't cease to be, and it's for that reason that God must incarcerate wicked and unruly spirits in hell. If he didn't He would have spirits causing trouble all over the universe. That's the reason hell was created, it wasn't made just to punish us out of some sense of macabre pleasure on God's part, it actually had to be a place that was appropriate to hold the power of the unregenerated spirit beings that God had created. People say well if God new they would go bad why did he make them? Well God is all about allowing choice which incidentally is a good rule for a happy relationship in your home as well.

You see a spirit being lives eternally and cannot die. If the spirit is not submissive to God in love and has not been regenerated and made alive in God, has not been born again, or whatever terminology you would choose to use, then we would have an unruly, basically evil spirit, who was now not subject to the light limit on the earth. And so what we would have in fact is thousands of satans (a mass demonic plague if you like) causing chaos in the universe.

The light limit is the barrier God has put on the earth to keep the natural and the spirit world apart. Science tells us that particles vibrating at the speed of light 186,000 miles a second will cause solid objects in this world to disappear, and not just to the sight you can feel for them and they are gone. Similarly when God wants an Angel to come into our world he just slows down below that limit and we can then see him. This might sound strange if you've never heard about this before but there have been many studies done on such things. If you would like to know more I'm sure you could look up experiments using electromagnetic fields where they have made things completely disappear and at times had them reappear in different places, and you would be able to discover more on the subject. God on the other hand is really well versed on the subject and shows us a little with incidents such as Jesus getting in the boat in the lake and immediately making the boat be at the other side of the lake.

> **19. "So when they had rowed about five and twenty or thirty furlongs, they see Jesus walking on the sea, and drawing nigh unto the ship: and they were afraid."**
>
> **20. "But he saith unto them, it is I, be not afraid,"**
>
> **21. "Then they willingly received him into the ship: and immediately the ship was at the land wither they went." (Jn. 6 v 19-21)**

This type of thing may seem a little bit like science fiction but we've been so spiritually ignorant of the things of God that, just like the Pharisees when they encountered Jesus, didn't even recognize Him as the Word that they professed to believe. Another example can be found in the book of Acts where Philip had just preached to the eunuch and had baptized him;

> **39. "and when they where come up out of the water, the Spirit of the Lord caught away Philip, that the eunuch saw him no more: and he went on his way rejoicing."**
>
> **40. "But Philip was found at Azotus: and passing through he preached in all the cities, till he came to Caesarea." (Acts. 8 v 39-40)**

The Bible tells us that the Lord caught away Philip and put him in another place. We don't hear much if anything in churches about scripture like these or even about scripture as in first John where he says to us;

17. "Herein is our love made perfect, that we may have boldness in the Day of Judgment: because as he is so are we in this world." (1Jn. 4 v 17)

It seems that these scriptures are too bold or too controversial for people to preach on with any sort of confidence. If we limit God's ability and wonders through a lack of faith in our world, we will limit God in our life, and therefore limit our life to only that which our minds can comprehend.

Ok so we see in **Luke chapter six verse forty five** that a good man or a bad person will bring good or bad out of the abundance of the Heart. What's in your spirit in abundance is what will come out. Not just what's in there but what's in there in the biggest quantity. So what's being said here is this, you could have lots of God's word in your heart and maybe you might go to church three times a week. You may run a prayer meeting for the church and have a house group going but if you have something in your heart more than those things, then that's what will come out. If you did all that though, you would probably have the Word in there in abundance any way, but the principal still remains because Jesus said it's true. If you have lots of Word but more worry, it's worry that will rise first in a crisis.

A lot of Christians get caught with this, they say "I've been good", and they have. "I go to church" and they do. "I read my Bible" and that's right too but it says what's there in abundance is what you will rely on. If your more convinced in medication help than you are in the healing power of the word you can talk the talk but when the pressure comes on you will automatically go for the meds. It's just a fact of human nature, the natural man's conditioning without the revelation of healing.

This is why it is so important to guard your heart or your spirit man from religious stories and from unbelief and doubt. If you sit in a church that continually feeds your spirit with condemnation preaching and guilt, always talking about being sinners saved by grace instead of being the righteousness of God in Christ Jesus, then when pressure comes on you in a situation you will doubt God's desire to help you and it will be hard for you to receive.

Jesus said out of the treasure or the input you have stored up in your spirit you will bring forth things. Things will come into your life according to what you say out of that treasure, because he says, "out of that abundance of the heart the mouth speaks". So basically what you say is what you will bring into your life.

We've looked at it in terms of a faith confession but here God is showing us the principal in regard to guarding what goes in, because what is in there is what issues are going to come in the outflow or the issues of life that preserve you here on this earth. So now can you see why God says to us as a loving parent, to watch what goes into your spirit? If you put in stories, soap opera television shows, fictional lessons, and or perverse thoughts and so on you will only have the power that stuff can generate in the universe to sustain your body and mind in this world. Some may say, "Well we eat food to keep our bodies going." Well tell that to the man dying of cancer or the person who's contemplating suicide out of severe depression. Your car runs on petrol, that's its food, but the fuel is no good to it if the thing falls to bits in the drive way.

Faith filled words based on what God has already stated, that the Spirit of life in Christ Jesus, will as we've seen from Romans, dominates the law of sin and death. God gave us dominion and Jesus gave it back to us again and God wants us to walk in that freedom from fear, injury, sickness and death so He says guard your spirit and be healthy.

Proverbs four again;

22. "For they are life unto those that find them and health to all their flesh." (Prov. 4 v 22)

Here we see again that God's Word equals health and life to all who find them. Keeping God's words in our heart will keep us on track with a real life. In fact if you're not healthy you really don't have much of a life anyway. If your heart is full of the Word of God then there won't be much room for or time to spend on the things that clog up your spiritual arteries and cause us to become spiritually unfit.

1. "My son, forget not my law: but let thine heart keep my commandments:"

2. "For length of days, and long life, and peace, shall they add to thee." (Prov. 3 v 1-2)

Nobody I've ever talked to that wasn't very ill, either physically or mentally, has said to me that they wanted to die. Well here in this fourth proverb God has given us a recipe for health and well being, and if we follow it, stay in the Word and guard your heart, your spirit man, following God's recipe, it will work for your wellbeing. Not guarding your heart could hinder your chances of success in this life.

Healing belongs to you, it's part of your inheritance it is why Jesus took that horrific belting for you and I and **God's will is to do it for you**.

Chapter Thirteen

The Ministry of Angels

> **14. "Are they not all ministering spirits,
> Sent forth to minister for them who shall be
> heirs of salvation?" (Heb. 1v14)**

THERE HAS BEEN much written said and painted about Angels, most of it a load of rubbish. People are educated in many ways and according to what manner or method you were educated, will to a large degree determine your beliefs. If you have been educated or taught of Angels by the art world for instance you may have the opinion that Angels are little fat babies with bows and arrows or perhaps a very thin effeminate male figure with long wavy hair. If your knowledge of Angels came from those that consider themselves to be spiritualists or mediums of the spirit world, you may believe that Angels are spirit guides, long blond haired women, or something that looks decidedly Gothic and so on. In just the same way our children grow up to often following in our footsteps, and with our beliefs. A Doctors child for instance feels that he wants to be a Doctor or a Preachers child will follow in the belief that people need God and a factory or social workers child may grow up to do the same job. This is quite normal because the Bible says to us that;

> **6. "Train a child up in the way he
> should go: and when he is old, he will
> not depart from it." (Prov. 22 v 6)**

We can see here that God tells us that we learn as we grow, in other words the things and the way that we are educated with in relation to a subject is the way that we are going to believe about it. If your children hear you talking of the virtues of preaching or the satisfaction of teaching students it is likely they will take an interest and develop the same belief and therefore want naturally to follow that path. So if people are told all their lives that Angels are this or that and that they operate in this or that fashion, then that information is what they will operate on, just as some people believe that God is mad at them all the time. They have been told that as they grew physically and in spiritual ignorance until some of them would and do defend their religious beliefs unto death. (Yours or theirs)

The Word tells us that the Angels are Ministering Spirits; this word means that the Angels are to minister as would a public servant, in that they serve us with a specific appointment to duty. That appointment comes from God the Father in relation to looking after us as their charges. Some people first of all don't even believe that there are Angels let alone in our midst, let alone here to actually help us and if you implied for one second that these Angels were in any way to actually obey anything we were to say or instruct them to do, they would think you were crazy or just a stupid big headed spiritually proud person talking rubbish.

The church world for centuries has grown up teaching that Angels are mythological beings that fly around heaven and occasionally have contact with humans, by appearing as the afore mentioned woman with blond curly hair to comfort some poor soul about to be thrown to the lions, and depicted as such in many a painting. The church world propagated this image of Angels by accepting such pictures depicting Angels as either females, babies or effeminate male, so called, Angelic beings, and placing them in prominent places in our churches and cathedrals for people to see and thus educating people in that direction in relation to the way Angels looked. This in turn gave us our adjective term to be, "angelic" meaning gentle, pretty, kind and with some mystical sense of heaven about them.

The term is probably best recognized when used in relation to looks or complexion, the doe eyes and the peaches and cream colouring of the facial skin, where we say, she or he has an angelic look about them.

We have been so interested about what Angels have looked like that we've given little thought to the really important questions of what should we consider about these beings, what if anything does God say about them and can we interact with them and if so on what level?

20. "Bless the Lord, ye his Angels that excel in strength, that do his commandments hearkening unto the voice of his word." (Pslm. 103 v 20)

Notice the wording here, remember earlier I said, one of the first things that God ever told me as a minister was to read what's actually there not what someone else said was written in the word. Here He says to us that Angels listen or hearken, which really implies they listen and act on the instruction. They hearken to, now look at this it's important, to the voice of His Word, not His voice, but to the voice of His Word. Now of course they would act on God's own word but what God is saying here as with other scriptures in the Word where truth is hidden for us not from us, is that the Angels listen to, and move on and at, the sound of God's Word. That means that when your voice is saying God's Word, they will hearken (hear and act) on it.

Now I realize that this may sound a little presumptuous as did some of the other things I've shared. It took me a little while to come to terms with it, just as it did the fact that I was righteous, but the fact remains, we are acknowledged as such by God through the shed Blood of the Lamb and this fact is no different. If God says a thing is so then it is so and you are not reprimanded for believing Him. If it is something that is really off then the Lord through the ministry of the Holy Ghost as Teacher will correct us on it and put us on the right track. But there are many powerful ministries in the earth teaching these things and there are many accounts of Angels intervening in people's lives who have operated on this revelation.

When Oral Roberts was told by Jesus to build a hospital he said, "Ok, but where will I get the money," Jesus said "I'll provide it through your faith," so again he said "Ok" and Jesus told him that the Angel in the room with them was there to help him get it. When brother Roberts said "Why is he still standing there?" Jesus said "He is waiting for you to send him." So at the Lord's instruction he sent the Angel to work in Jesus name.

I believe it was an Angel that barred the door to the hairdresser's shop the day the Lord told me to go and get a haircut and pray with the hairdresser. On another occasion I was attacked by a man intending to do me no good at all and when he got to within a step of me he suddenly flipped over and rolled on the ground. He didn't know what happened to him but I did; my Angel made sure that he **"touched not the Lord's anointed and do his prophet no harm." (1Chr. 16v2**) And that's exactly what happened.

On another occasion I was jogging for exercise as is my habit and I inadvertently got between an old man and his German Shepherd Dog. The dog obviously thought I was a threat to his master and came straight at me with teeth snarling. It was very hard to keep my composure and I do believe if I had doubted at all or panicked and ran the outcome would have been very different. As it was I held my nerve and trusted God believing He would help in the name of Jesus, for things to be ok.

Just as the dog was about ten meters away I heard a voice inside my head say "Not yet just wait." Somehow I instinctively knew that I was to wait for God to move, as the dog, the big dog and it was big believe me, jumped at me, I heard this voice say "Now," as I heard the voice it was as if my leg shot out by itself and I kicked the dog in the chest lifting him over in a clean summersault, a full back flip, where upon he turned and ran back to the owner who immediately apologized for his dog's behavior and continued on. Now in the first place that dog must have weighed twenty five kilos if he weighed a gram and there was no way I could have kicked him over like that, and even if I did have that power it would have broken his ribs for sure. No I believe again it was an Angel who intervened on my behalf.

There have been other incidents where things that seemed impossible suddenly were happening, times where my own human strength alone was not enough and then, suddenly people I was working with would be astonished at my strength to lift or move something that was really obviously too heavy to move by myself, and yet it happened. Again I believe that an Angel helped me do what needed to be done. When I have a situation like that I say "Lord I need your strength for this, mine is not enough" and then I just do what is necessary.

The Bible tells us that;

> 7. "The Angel of the Lord encampeth round about them that fear him, and delivereth them." (Pslm. 34 v 7)

The Word promises us that if we fear or reverence and have respect for God then the Angels will surround us and deliver us or keep us safe from harm. This is the protection from physical as well as spiritual injury in this world that God affords us.

> 10. "There shall no evil befall thee, neither shall any plague come nigh thy dwelling."
>
> 11. "For he shall give his Angels charge over thee to keep thee in all thy ways." (Pslm. 91 v 10-11)

Notice that we are promised protection and safety because of the charge to these beings by God. They are charged with our welfare but as with everything else in God we need to believe Him for it. We must be in faith and confess we have the ministry of Angels to keep us safe at all times in all circumstances.

This leads us to what exactly an Angel is, they are warriors of God, beings created by God that are neither male or female that is neither given or taken in marriage the Bible says **(Matt. 22 v 30)** and who are supremely capable of fighting for you in the spirit world and remember, the Word said that "they excel in strength" so they are well able to protect you in this physical world.

They are not little fat babies or girls or girly boys they are Soldiers of Heaven, created beings who obey the Word of the Lord without question and who, we we're told, obey the voice of the Word when we use it. They are ministering spirits who minister for the heirs of salvation, that's us folks. As with everything else we're not flippant about it or irreverent about these things of God, but never the less it is He who told us that these things operate this way so let's take the revelation and run with it.

The Prophet Elisha was in a bit of a situation at one time in **11 Kings**, and his servant was very worried about the outcome, for it seemed as though they may be harmed. The Prophet did this;

> 17. "And Elisha prayed and said, Lord, I pray thee, open his eyes that he may see. And the Lord opened the eyes of the young man; and he saw: and, behold, the mountain was full of horses and chariots of fire round about Elisha." (11 Kings. 6v22)

Elisha prayed that his servant might see the Angelic protection that God had in place for them so he would not be afraid. Just because you can't see the Angels doesn't mean they're not there.

> 10. "Take heed that ye despise not one of these little ones; for I say unto you, that in heaven their Angels do always behold the face of my Father which is in heaven." (Matt. 18v10)

We talk often of children having Angels to watch over them, most of the time it is said just to comfort them without people really believing it. Jesus tells us here that it was so, that the Angels of the children were before the face of the Father. Well when Jesus said "Our Angels were in heaven" and at that time, should they be sent to help us, they needed to battle satanic forces to get through on what was called Jacob's ladder. **(Dan. 10 v 12-13)** Well Jesus defeated all the satanic forces in hell and took authority over them. When it came time to ascend to heaven after His resurrection, He had no trouble doing it. He did not have to battle the demonic forces, they couldn't hinder Him anymore, because He had already done that and as such the Angels that were before the face of the Father then, and now, have no trouble in going backwards and forwards, and in fact it says in Hebrews that they have been sent; but nowhere does it say that they have left. So the Angels that were there then representing us are now right here with us protecting and helping us in this life.

We all have a personal Angel when we are small children but he didn't leave when we grew up, we are still God's children and as far as he's concerned we're still worth protecting. That's why the Word says that "They are ministering spirits sent forth," they've been sent forth to look after us, to look after God's children like caretakers. Some of the doubt in regard to this fact may be related again to a righteousness consciousness in that we have misinterpreted scripture and taught it as gospel.

I pointed out before that there was a causative and permissive verb in the Hebrew language that we needed to consider, well there is also the factor of the translators feeling uncomfortable with the truth and struggling with a lack of righteousness consciousness themselves as do many today. In the Book of Psalms we read;

> **4. "What is man that thou art mindful of him?**
> **And the son of man, that thou visitest him?"**
>
> **5. "For thou hast made him a little**
> **lower than the angels, and hast crowned**
> **him with glory and honour."**

The translators here have rightly said that God has crowned us with glory and honour but what they just didn't have the nerve to write was the correct word that the original Hebrew stated. For in the original it says, "That God made man a little lower than Eloheem" another word for deity or The Trinity. God had said He made man a little lower than Himself. Genesis tells us that we were made in the image and likeness of God Himself and that He gave us dominion over the works of His hand.

> **6. "Thou madest him to have dominion**
> **over the works of thy hands; thou hast put**
> **all things under his feet;" (Pslm. 8 v 6)**

Angels are the works of His hand just as the earth is. The people that have a problem with accepting that they are the righteousness of God in Christ Jesus also have a problem accepting the authority that goes along with that, and so have a problem believing that the Angels are sent to minister for us, it doesn't say "To minister to us", it says "They minister for us."

Some would still argue that in the book of **Jude v 9** he said that when disputing over Moses body with the devil even Michael the Archangel said, "The Lord rebuke you" because even he had no authority to say otherwise, but that was before Jesus went to the cross. After He went to the cross He gave us all authority over the devil and told us to go in His name cast out devils, heal the sick and take the Gospel of love, power and peace and tell the world that God now wants to do for them. That's why it's called Good News.

In the Old Testament and the Gospels you must remember everything is actually done under the Old Testament Covenant. Jesus hadn't gone to the cross yet and had not brought the New Covenant into existence, and with it the authority given to us by him in which we now stand by faith. If you remember that fact it will help with a lot of things that give people cause to hesitate at the promises and wonder about some of the teachings. When Jesus hung on the cross one of the things He said was that "It is finished". Again you could ask ten Christians what He meant and you'd probably get more than a few different answers depending on their teaching. What He was talking about was the Old Covenant, it was the Old Covenant that was finished and He was about to ratify the new one with better promises and more authority.

When God made mankind a little lower than Himself it was so as to make us as close to equal as He could to Himself without us being in his place, which is what the devil wanted and which got him kicked out of heaven in the first place. God goes to great lengths all the way through the Bible to continually reassure us of who we are, with statements like; we are the Body of Christ, let this mind be in you that was in Christ who being in the form of God thought it not robbery to be equal with God, for their righteousness is of me saith the Lord, and if you be Christ's then you are Abraham's seed and heirs according to the promise. That promise is the promise to see and treat us as though we had never sinned and so on. All these statements and many more attest to the fact that God has set us above all else in creation in the blood of Christ and that we should also accept that we are above Angels, who the Bible tells us desire to look into this mystery, that is our New Birth in Christ. Think it not wrong with this in mind that God would allow your the help of the Angels at you request in faith.

Speaking of Jesus the writer of Hebrews says of Jesus;

> **3. Who being the brightness of his glory, and the express image of his person, and upholding all things by the word of his power, when he had by himself purged our sins, sat down on the right hand of the Majesty on high;"**
>
> **4. "Being made so much better than the Angels, as he has by inheritance obtained a more excellent name than they."**
>
> **5. "For unto which of the Angels said he at any time, Thou art my son, this day have I begotten thee? And again, I will be to him a Father, and he shall be to me a son?"**
>
> **6. "And again, when he bringeth in the first begotten into the world, he saith, and let all the angels of God worship him." (Heb. 1 v 3-6)**

Notice the Word here tells us that Jesus is acknowledged as being made so much better than the Angels, He's been given a better name and God has instructed the Angels to worship Him because He is again a son to Him. The reason that God said, "He is again a son" was because at the cross Jesus died. People as I mentioned before will accept that He died physically but debate whether He died spiritually. We must let Him die spiritually in our thinking or else He cannot be our substitute in that regard. Now here we see that God says to us that again Jesus is become a son to Him, because at some point He must have been lost to God. That was at the time God had to let Him go spiritually. Notice here also that God has called Him the first begotten, that's the first one re-born from the dead under the new covenant; and at some point you were re-born if you are a Christian believer, and so you too have a number in there. Jesus was first born so He is number one, yours and my number may be in the thousands and thousands but it is still in there, we have a number recorded in God the second, the third, the hundred millionth, whatever, but it is recognized by God as the number of one of His children just as He did for Jesus;

> 4. "But God, who is rich in mercy, for his great love wherewith he loved us,"
>
> 5. "Even when we were dead in sins, hath quickened us together with Christ, (by grace ye are saved)."
>
> 6." And hath made us sit together in heavenly places in Christ Jesus:"
>
> 7. "That in the ages to come he might shew the exceeding riches of his grace in his kindness toward us through Christ Jesus." (Eph. 2 v 4-7)

God has said the Angels should worship Jesus because He is God's own son with an inherited position, not as a servant as are they. Now Jesus always has preeminence because He's the head of the Body of Christ but God has told us in many places in the Bible that we are his children, sons of God. That we are joint heirs etc, so that even though it doesn't ever put us above Christ it certainly gives us preeminence over the Angels. Furthermore God has said to us that He wants to show us the exceeding riches of his love towards us in the ages to come. He doesn't make those promises to the Angels and anywhere in the Bible an Angel appears before a man, if the man kneels to worship him the Angel says not to do it. Anyone who claims to have been visited by Jesus Himself such as Oral Roberts or Kenneth E Hagin have all told us that as they fell, bowed or knelt before Him He always told them to stand or lifted them up in His presence. God the Father, Jesus and the Angels all respect the position that God has decreed that the re-born man holds in the Kingdom of God. A Position that the Angels themselves Peter tells us, desire to look into **(1 Pet. V 12)**. Note also that **(Eph. 2 v 6)** tells us that we are made to sit together in heavenly places in Christ. The Angels are worshiping, falling at the feet of Jesus saying worthy is the Lamb of God that was slain, but we are sitting in heaven in Christ. We will be worshiping our God but the terminology used to explain things to us shows us that we are on a completely different level to the Angels, magnificent as they are they are not sons and daughters of God in Christ but we are. So don't doubt that these incredible beings the servants of God will help, minister to and protect you, on the charge that God has given them. The Bible tells us in **(1Corinthians 6 v 3)** that we shall judge Angels, not that Angels judge us, that we judge them; the lesser does not judge the greater but visa versa.

I asked the Lord one day after He had reminded me of the fact that I had a personal Angel watching over me, if I could meet him, He said, "No not yet because if you see him you will trust in him more than you will me. You will call on him before me because you will believe what you see more than what you don't see." I said "Ok Lord I can understand that," but He left me with the impression on my mind that someday when I am not moved at all by what I see but by only what I believe, He will introduce me to him.

We have a personal Angel and there are multitudes of other Angels who operate at the command of God and to the voice of His Word. They bring us messages they help us physically, and I'm sure they take care of things we haven't discovered yet. Friends of mine told me once that neighbours had come to them asking, "Who were the people in white clothes standing on their lawn at night?" My friends told them they were the Angels that protected their home and lives. These people believed in the ministry of Angels and confessed them working and protecting in their lives.

The Bible makes hundreds of references to the existence of Angels and to their presence in our midst. God has provided them for a ministry to us, those of whom are called heirs of salvation. It is God's idea that they do their job for us and they are happy to be serving God doing his bidding and harkening to the voice of His Word. The Angels will also figure heavily in the last days the bible talks about them gathering the saints, sifting those that are from those that aren't or only look as though they are. That again though is their ministry to the saints, a provision of God's love for them in the end times. This though is relative to the Jewish people and those who are saved after the rapture. I'll explain this more in the chapter entitled what happens at the end. God said they will minister for you; He will make sure because of His love for us, that they do. Believe it. **God's will is to do it for you.**

Chapter Fourteen

The Names reflect the Nature of God

> 1. "O Give thanks unto the Lord; call upon his name: Make known His deeds among the people." (Plsm.105v1)

> 8. "Our help is in the Name of the Lord, Who made Heaven and Earth." (Pslm. 124v8)

CALL UPON THE name of the Lord is the encouragement and instruction to us here. Call upon Him for help and because of His great deeds. The Lord is indeed mighty and His name is worthy to call upon. It has been said by the poet that a Rose by any other name would smell as sweet, implying that the name is of little or no importance to the value and beauty of the Rose. That may very well be true of the Rose but when the name is the Lord God Almighty the name becomes significantly more important.

We give names to things, people and places etc. so as we can identify, catalogue and have reference points in relation to them and what they are. We understand what something or someone can do in relation to us by the name we have given it. The Bible also teaches that naming rights also identifies authority but that's another teaching and I'm not dealing with that here. It is a subject worth looking into if you are interested in walking in the authority God has given you. God gave us the right to name the things on the earth, the animals, the plants, the fish etc. However He enlightened us through the ministry of the Holy Spirit to men as to what we should call Him.

God provides for us on the basis of His love for us and through the avenue of faith. We must receive everything we get from God by faith as I've explained before, so as to keep the evil one's hands out of it. God revealed to us what His names are or what we should address Him as at different times depending on what it was we needed. He did the same thing and for the same reasons when He was dealing with Abram, by renaming him Abraham. In that way every time Abram said his name he was confessing the thing he wanted to happen. In his case it was to be a Father. God too tells us to call Him different Names at different times depending on our need because the names of God reflect His giving nature.

When we have a need of provision we know and confess the Lord as **Jehovah-Jireh,** which to us now means and implies that it is God who provides for us. Jehovah Jireh our provider. Abraham gave that name to the place where God provided a ram as the substitute for his son (the lamb came later in the form of Jesus) Yahweh yireh which means "The Lord provides." In confessing that God is Jehovah Jireh we are saying that God provides and on that confession of our faith God will provide for us.

Many years ago when my children were small I had occasion to come under attack in relation to our finances. We were producing a magazine called the witness and an instruction paper called Insight which we distributed in Churches schools and anywhere people would receive them. At this particular time we were very short of food and so I went to God to ask about our provision and why we were struggling because He had told me once that provision is already there you are just missing it. I said to the Lord "Jesus I know that you have provided for us I believe that and your Word says that **you have not seen the righteous forsaken or his seed begging bread." (Pslm. 27v35)** I decided to go for a walk and pray about this and wait on the Lord. I often find it easier to be still or to cope if the pressure is on by walking outside in the freshness and sunshine. I did this for a day or so and I couldn't understand why the answer hadn't come to me. Each day my walk would end with me strangely enough at the shops near the beach where I was living at the time.

As if things weren't pressing enough I would end up at the same spot every day and that was with my face looking into the Bakery window at all the food on sale for the people with money to spend.

Unfortunately at that time that wasn't me. I was very tempted each day to just go in and ask for some food. It wasn't as though we had no food at all for the children or I might have but we just had some rice, flour and sugar that sort of thing. Not anything to make a really substantial meal out of. Well each day I would find myself at this shop it was as if I were drawn to it by something. I just put it down to being hungry at first but then I remembered something I heard a while before from Kenneth Copeland while he was preaching on prosperity, he said something along the lines that, as you make yourself a channel of God and the provision for others comes through you there will always be enough for you; as a laborer is worthy of his hire. Just then it hit me what God was trying to get through to me

The next day knowing of the great need out in the community already I wrote to all of the bakeries in our area and asked them if I could pick up the food left over at the end of the day. They agreed I could with some provisos in relation to reheating and storage etc. and so that night I picked up about four large bakery trays from the first bakery. It was full of pies and cakes of all kinds. In the days and weeks that followed there seemed to be more and more left over each week. Others that were collecting for other groups no longer wanted it so I was able to feed people far and wide in my community which at the time was the western beaches area of Adelaide. By the time I moved on there was around three thousand dollars worth of food available to us on any given day, and needless to say we always had some-thing to eat ourselves. God's provision was there already, I just had to see it and keep my confession of Jehovah Jireh our provider. It was in the giving.

Jehovah Raphah, the word Raphah means to mend or to heal. God said He sent His Word and healed them **(Pslm. 107v20)** His love for us caused Him to send the Word that healed us and we've already seen how Jesus was the Word made flesh so as to dwell amongst us and teach and heal us. God has promised us deliverance and help in all we do Moses built an Alta and called the place **Yahweh nissi** The Lord is my banner. A banner is a standard and by that I mean it is a sign of who we are and which side or power we represent. A banner or standard is held aloft in battle to signify our country, these days we call it a flag. Under this flag we supposedly have all the rights and resources of whatever or whoever is represented by that flag or standard.

When Moses erected an Alta to God and called the place The Lord is my banner, he was saying under the Lord I am entitled to all the protection and resource that God has at His disposal. You see God and His Word are one and He said that Jesus is the Word and we are in Jesus. What this tells us is that God is our banner He is our standard. Under Him we are entitled to Love safety and protection. As we confess what He has put in the mind of man to say about Him again it will come to pass in our lives. **Jehovah Nissi** our banner of protection.

All that we have from God is available to us because God can now accept us as His children. This fact has come about because of the fact that God is **Jehovah tsidkenu** from "Yahweh sidqenu" meaning The Lord our Righteousness. God is righteousness and has made us so out of His great care and affection for us. The nature of God is to continually give and love and forgive.

Jehovah shalom means the Lord is peace. He doesn't have peace He is peace just as He doesn't have love for us He is love toward us. It's not a conditional thing that changes with circumstance or opportunity as with man. It is what He is and He is toward us all the time. When Jesus was born on earth the Angel declared "Peace on earth good will toward mankind." That was God's message I have good will toward you. All my will is to send good toward you.

The names associated with God are a reflection of His nature and a sign to us that He is available to us in that name and for what it represents. Some of the other names that can be associated with God and appropriated by faith by us to our blessing are;

You will be able to see from the names where you by faith can receive from God on the basis of the name and what it represents.

"**Jehovah shammah**" Yahweh samma, The Lord is there, so where is there? Everywhere you are.

"**The Lord of Hosts**" Yahweh sabot, Lord of all heavens Angelic armies and power.

"**The Lord God of Israel**" Yahweh lohe yisrael, The Lord of Abraham Isaac and Jacob Lord God of the living.

"**The Holy One of Israel**" Qdos yisrael representing strength and might.

"**Ancient of Days**" Aram attiq yomin representative of the Most High God on His throne judging the world empires.

And of course as Christ to us;

The Almighty, He is the Alpha and Omega the beginning and the end, He is our Advocate in heaven, He is the Apostle and High Priest of our confession, the Arm of the Lord, the Author and finisher of our faith, the Blessed and only Potentate, He is the Branch and the Vine into which we are all grafted, He is the Bread of life, Captain of the Hosts of heaven, He is the Chief Shepherd and the Christ of God.

He is the Chief Corner Stone, the Commander and Counsellor; He is the Day Spring, the Deliverer and the Desire of all Nations. His is the Door by which men can be saved. He is the Elect, Emanuel, (God with us), Eternal Life and the Everlasting Father. He is the Faithful Witness, the First and the Last and the First Born from the dead. He's the Good Shepherd, the Head of the Church and the Heir of all things. He is the Holy One of Israel, the Great I am and Jehovah. He is the King of the Saints, King of the Jews and King of Kings. The Lamb of God, he is Life, Light, the Lord of Glory and the Lion of the Tribe of Judah. He's the Mediator between God and Man, the Messenger of the New Covenant and the Morning Star, Jesus is the Prince of Life, the Prince of Peace and the Redeemer of Mankind. He is the Prophet and was the Ransom for Mankind, He is the Resurrection and the life, and He is the Savior, the Servant and the Bishop of our Souls. He's the Son of God, the Son of Man and the Sun of Righteousness. He is the Truth the Life and the Way. He is Wonderful, He is The Witness, The Word and He is my personal Savior. He is Jesus Christ of Nazareth. Hallelujah!

As I said in the title of this chapter the names of God reflect the nature of God. God's nature is to give. He is love, light, Peace, Joy, Salvation and everything else we know Him for, but His nature is one of giving. You can see from the names that God wants us to see Him as a loving Father. It should be clearly evident to you reading this book by now that God has had a lot of things projected on to Him in regard to what He will do or won't do. He wants us to see Him as loving so that we will come to the throne of Grace confident that He will meet our needs. The Names tell us that He will. **God's will is to do it for you.**

Chapter Fifteen

What Happens at "The End"

> 12. "And I saw the dead small and
> great, stand before God;"
> And the books were opened: and
> another book was opened,"
> Which is the book of life: and
> the dead were judged
> Out of those things which were
> written in the books,
> According to their works." (Rev. 20v12)

I DON'T THINK I've ever spoken to a person (who isn't a teacher of the Word of some kind) that isn't a bit confused and a little worried about what is going to happen to them at the end of the world. If the person is a teacher of the Bible and that doesn't mean their correct in what they say, as there are a lot of really strange beliefs being shared on all sorts of subjects these days, but they usually have a particular view on what they think is going to happen should they still be alive when the world ends and the Lord returns, and so for them there is some measure of comfort in that belief. Unless of course they are those of the persuasion that believe they must go through some terrible tribulation or some kind of purgatory before they are redeemed by God. This thinking is usually accompanied by a doctrinal belief that warrants some penalty, sacrifice, or penance other than what Christ has already paid at Calvary for them. Generally though most Christians I've ever met are really confused as to what is going to happen. Most of them just hope firstly that they will be able to live out their lives before the terrible things that they may have heard about come on the earth in the latter times and if that is possible, that they are accepted into heaven when their time comes to leave this place. They don't seem to have a clear description of the events that will happen, how they will happen or an understanding of the order of those events, so as to feel secure about that which will, one day surely be upon them.

I am going to share some information with you in this chapter that will hopefully give you some understanding of the events to come, so as to give your heart some rest, trusting in the promises of a loving God, who has already made provision for you to be delivered from the fearsome end of the world and the great battle of Armageddon that is to come. Firstly I want you to look at a scripture in Galatians speaking of Jesus says;

> **4. "Who gave himself for our sins, that he might deliver us from this present evil world, according to the will of God and our Father." (Gal. 1 v 4)**

The scripture says we have been delivered from this world. Now you may say "Well that has to be a metaphor or is meant just in a spiritual sense because we are still physically here." Well that's correct but we still believe we have our redemption in Christ even though we are still standing on the earth. We understand that it is agreed to in heaven so that when the time comes that we need to have that manifest it will happen. We put faith in the fact that God will keep His Word because He cannot lie and that He will take us when our physical life ends and we leave the body. Well this scripture tells us that we have been delivered, just as the Bible tells us that we are saved, it takes the same faith, it's the same word given by the same God, so why see it in a different light with different criteria? This scripture tells us we have been delivered, the word <u>might</u> in this verse doesn't mean He may or may not, it means so that He qualified to save us and take us out.

The Amplified Bible which explains a little more into the original translations for clarity puts it this way;

> **4. "Who gave (yielded) Himself up (to atone) for our sins (and to save and sanctify**

> us), in order to rescue and deliver us from this present wicked age and world order, in accordance with the will and purpose and plan of our God and Father." (Gal. 1 v 4)

The will, purpose and plan of our Father is to rescue, deliver, save etc us from this world order and wicked age. Why if that was His plan would He as some people fear, leave you here to face the most horrific times the world has ever known. What would be the purpose of Christ facing the cross for the deliverance of the church, if it wasn't going to happen? Some may say "Oh that was so we could go to heaven after the tribulation is all over." Well it says to rescue us from this wicked age and world order, if we had to wait until it's all over what do we need rescuing from?

Now I'm not intending to give you a detailed study of all the scripture and events significant to the end times, but rather an overview of events. If you find your interest is sparked you can always find information about Bible prophecy from books, any Mainline, or Pentecostal Church or a reputable Christian Bible College. (I would suggest however that you don't study end time prophecy from a sect that claims they are the chosen few). For me to detail where all the information came from to come to the conclusions I have come to and the opinions I hold in regard to End Times Events, I would have to go into great detail, into the books of Daniel, Ezekiel, Revelation, also Prophetic ministries I have studied under myself, personal revelation and the Gospels; so as I said at the opening I want to give you an overview of events that will give you a more settled understanding of what God has in store for us.

I remember for years, every time I started to feel ok about end time events someone would say or teach something that would frighten me really badly about what was coming in the end. I was always left feelling a little unsure about my fate. Even though I believed I was going to heaven, I was niggled with the thoughts that I would have to be killed or worse because of the old seventies teachings about Christian persecutions, where women and children would be portrayed in movies having their heads cut off while trying to buy food because they were Christians.

I know that people all over the world are persecuted for the faith all the time, and I myself would rather die as far as I know than to deny my Lord, but we are talking here about a belief in a worldwide persecution of everybody that does not carry "the mark of the beast." Any person that professes to follow Christ in the way of the true church will be executed or some such thing. I personally don't believe that this understanding is at all correct.

There are three main theories as to what will happen in general at the end of time as we know it, Pre, Mid and Post Tribulation described as follows. One group of people believe that the Bible teaches that all believers will have to go through all of whatever is coming on the earth, and that if they hold their confession right to the end in the face of all the persecution, the plagues and the famines and if they hold through the last great war called Armageddon, either living or not then when Jesus returns they will finally be safe. This is called post tribulation redemption. They go after.

The second theory is that in the tribulation, (the name given to all the afore told events of the last days for reference sake, that is made up of two periods of three and a half years, seven years in all). The Christians will only have to go through the first three and a half years (or mid tribulation) and not the second. In these two periods a lot of different events will take place some of which are that the grass gets burned up, the waters of the world are poisoned, that the sun becomes like blood, (sounds like pollution doesn't it?) That great famine will be upon the earth to the point where people will eat their own children, and that the people of the Jewish nation of Israel will be thrown into fiery ovens again (by the then ruler of the world who is called the Antichrist, for obvious reasons, he's anti anything to do with Christ), and that we will not as I mentioned be able to buy sell or exchange without accepting the mark of the beast.

The third theory (pre tribulation) and the one I personally believe, (and I'll show you why as we go along), is that God will take His people out of the earth before the major part of the seven year tribulation begins. Now I don't just belief or adhere to this theory because it sounds less frightening. I actually believe that God is a deliverer and that He is true to His word.

One of the reasons people get these events mixed up and misinterpret them is that they don't see that in some things God is talking about us as the Church, some places He is talking about the nation of Israel and the Jews, and in some instances He is talking about both of us, and occasionally He has a duel meaning in the scripture that relates differently to both parties. Of course sometimes He is talking about those that are in and of the world, those that are not born again children of God.

Now a lot of people may say that the Jews are not born again people so why do they get saved with the church? They don't. They are saved after the church but salvation is still for them because salvation Jesus said is of the Jews **(Jn.4v22)**. I realize I have made several statements here without scripture references but I'll give them to you I believe as I explain things along the way.

The hard part with giving an overview is that no matter where I start I'm going to be starting in the middle of something. This chain of events obviously started with Adam in the Garden and then moves on through Noah, the covenants and Abraham with the covenant God made with him to get Jesus into the earth, so He could go to the cross and pay the penalty for all sin. The Prophets of old confessed that there was one coming, that the Lord was coming, the soon coming King, the deliverer of Israel who would save the world from sin; and eventually the Bible tells us that the Word became flesh and dwelt among us Jesus was now in the earth. The end time clock was started and it's still running. It's my personal belief that in the course of world events in the light of prophecy and the events unfolding in the world today, that if the clock that began running when Jesus entered the earth was an alarm clock ready to signal the end, as an alarm clock does the end of your sleep in the mornings, this alarm clock has just had the button pop up as it does just before it rings. I believe we are that close to the last days events on the earth in terms of historical time before Jesus returns. I used to use the example of the old dynamite plunger, as it was pushed down there would be a couple of seconds before the bang, and in that stillness of the moment before the explosion there would be an intense anticipation, and it's that sense of anticipated urgency that I believe we should be living in today. We should, I believe be anticipating Christ's return and working accordingly on the things of God. There are still I believe many things yet to be fulfilled in Bible prophecy in terms of the end of the world, but not before the church can be raptured away in order to miss the tribulation. I believe that all prophecy that has to occur before the church can leave has already been fulfilled. It's now just a matter of the Lord's timing. So that's another reason I believe we need to get on with the job of getting people saved or supporting ministries that are.

Ok we now have Jesus in the earth and yes we've condensed about five thousand years of history into a couple of paragraphs I know, but I did say it was an overview. When Jesus began His ministry the Roman Empire was in power in Israel. There had been other powers that dominated Israel over the centuries like the Greeks and the Persians but the prophecies of the Old Testament Prophets had said that the Romans or the symbolism they used told us that it was those who called themselves the Roman Empire, would be the last great power to rule Israel before the judgment day or the end of the world as we know it. This confuses people because they say, "Well the Roman Empire is gone and we're not ever going to have a bunch of sword waving maniacs ruling the world again so how can this be?" Well If for a moment we take the arrival of Jesus on earth at that time out of the picture, the world for Israel would have gone on as prophesied and the Romans would have ruled until Jesus the Messiah came as a ruling King at the end of the world to deliver them, and destroy their enemies, which would have been the Romans and anybody else that had put themselves in that position by then.

The thing that changed all of that was the arrival of Jesus in the form of a man, which as we know from history was not an acceptable form as far as the Jewish people were concerned for their Messiah and so they rejected the notion that Jesus could be Him. However the Bible tells us that eventually He will show them the nail holes in His hands, and they will realize their mistake and worship Him for who He is, (just as He did for doubting Thomas);

> **7. "Behold he cometh with clouds; and every eye shall see him, and they also which pierced him; and all kindreds of the earth shall wail because of him Even so Amen." (Rev.1v7)**

Those clouds He comes in by the way I believe to be us the Church, because the Bible talks about clouds of righteousness and as we know the scriptures say we are the righteousness of God. Just another reason to believe we are not here while the trouble is going on at the end. How is it that we are there in the sky at this point? I'll tell you shortly.

When Jesus entered the earth, the normal course the world was on took a detour for a while. Again if I could use the analogy of the clock running for this specific period in time, the history clock has stopped for a while. This detour is what we call the church age it's the time from when Jesus came, until as I believe, He returns again in the sky and takes the church out of the earth before the tribulation. He will not set foot on the earth at this time for the trouble has yet to occur, but will wait until the appointed time and then return and destroy the enemies of Israel which by then will be many as you will see.

Jesus established the beginnings of the church through the Apostles, and subsequently it has grown over the years to where we are today. When Jesus left He ascended up on high went to heaven and sent the Holy Spirit to help us until His return for us. He is waiting now for that appointed time so He can come back and take all those that have believed on Him as their saviour. In the mean time while we are getting as many people saved as possible there are other events taking place that are fulfilling prophecy that was given thousands of years ago, and among them a lot of the events that we are seeing on the news Broadcasts lately.

> **6. "For many shall come in my name, saying I am Christ; and shall deceive many."**

> **7. "And when ye shall hear of wars and rumors of wars, be not troubled; for such things must needs be; but the end shall not be yet."**

> **8. "For nation shall rise against nation, and Kingdom against Kingdom: and there shall be earthquakes in divers places, and there**

> **shall be famines and troubles: these are the beginnings of sorrows." (Mk. 13 v 6-8)**

Some would say oh, we've always had wars and troubles somewhere and that's true, but we are having troubles no one had ever faced before in the history of the world, such as suicide bombers, earth quakes in the strangest places, 911, tsunamis, where millions of people are destroyed, well you watch the news you've seen it for yourself. Jesus said these are just the beginnings of the trouble. The tension is mounting all over the world steadily. There are counties who are not noted for their human rights, who now have very powerful weapons which they could turn on the rest of the world at any time, anyway you get the idea. We also have people claiming to be Christ; people like Jim Jones and David Koresh and who through some demonic power manage to convince people that they are actually the Christ reincarnate. Once the Lord of glory returns for His church, that's all those that have believed on His name, once they leave the historical clock will again begin to run.

It is at this point that the believers, the body of Christ will be taken before God for what is called Beamer judgment. This is not judgment of sins but judgment for reward. The Bible tell us as I've shown earlier in the book that we are passed from being judged unto death, unto life and so not judged for destruction. **(1 Jn. 3 v 14)**

Now had Jesus not come, I said the normal course of events would have occurred which meant the Romans would have still been in charge. The Bible tells us in the prophetic writings that there will be a one world Government and a One World Church in the end times, now this church is what the bible calls the "whore church," a whore is someone that is an adulterous, and the Bible calls the last days church, a whore because she adulterates the Word of God and builds herself on false teachings, fleshly ways and persecutes the Church that is here on the earth. **(Rev. Chapt. 17-18)**

These saints or members of the true church are those that have believed after the main body of believers has left the earth. The Bible tells us that there will be two prophets preaching the gospel at that time, we're not sure who they will be but the word says they will have fire comeing from their mouth **(Rev.chapt.11)**. They'll need that power at that time just to survive because once the church and the Holy Spirit have left the earth, hatred and evil will be the order of the day. The Government of the day will be a one world government with Antichrist at its head. There are prophetic writings which explain to the prophetically educated that this Antichrist led government has its headquarters in Rome on the seven hills. Remember I'm not giving you details of the prophetic writings just the bottom line basically. So this government led by Antichrist and supported by the "Whore Church" makes a deal with Israel allowing them to rebuild the temple in Jerusalem and begin their traditional worship again. Now you must remember that the Israelis' have been persecuted for hundreds of years not because they did anything wrong to anybody but because they are God's chosen people. They are the people that God made the covenants with, the people that our Lord came from. A lot of people in some denominations I know don't believe that God is saving the twelve tribes of Israel because of what the Jews did to Jesus, but that's not true as the Word tell us;

> **27. "Esaias also crieth concerning Israel, Though the number of the children of Israel be as the sand of the sea, a remnant shall be saved." (Rom. 9 v 27)**

Now again some religious cult members have said to me that this scripture refers not to Israel but to spiritual Israel. There are no references to spiritual Israel in the Bible. By spiritual Israel they mean themselves, who they consider to be the true church, the only church. You can always tell a cult I think when they tell you that they are the select few that are going to heaven based on some obscure teaching that has no basis in truth. When the Word says that salvation, "Is unto all and upon all them that believe" **(Rom. 3 v 22)** that's exactly what it means. I don't see how "unto all and upon all" could mean only those that follow a particular denomination's teaching are the only ones eligible to receive a place in heaven as I was told just recently by someone.

Antichrist who is revealed at the appointed time, allows Israel to take up their worship of God again as they did in the time that they were under the Roman rule of Jesus' time. Unfortunately for the Jewish people when they get their temple rebuilt Antichrist turns up and sits himself on the throne in the temple, and places Idols on the temple, probably little Idols of himself along with a Roman wing symbol, and demands that the Jewish nation worship him as lord, as did Nebuchadnezzar in the time of Daniel. Of course this infuriates the Israelis and they refuse just as did Shadrach, Meshach and Abednego, who were thrown into the fiery furnace for refusing to worship someone other than the God of Israel. As a result of this just as in the time of Daniel, Antichrist brings back a similar punishment and of course the Jews revolt. The Bible talks of the nations of the world gathering together under the banner of the false church and lead by the false prophet under the authority of the Antichrist himself against Israel. The countries are Gog and Magog that's Russia and China and the African nations and of course Europe led by the Antichrist himself out of Rome; which by now is the capital of the new world order, the one world Government and the one world church headquarters. The European forces are spoken about as the Ten Horned Beast, which is to be understood to be the ten nation confederation or as we know it the ten countries making up the common market of Europe the E.E.C. There will be twelve for a time but then drop back to ten. The forces combine and come against Israel in what the Bible says is a time like no other nor has ever been or ever will be.

> **21. "For then shall be great tribulation, such as was not since the beginning of the world to this time, no nor ever shall be." (Matt. 24 v 21)**

Antichrist by putting Idols on the temple and placing himself in the place reserved for the Lord God and defiles the temple and their worship which is called by Jesus, "the abomination of desolation."

> **15. "When ye therefore shall see the abomination of desolation spoken of by Daniel the prophet, stand in the holy place, whosoever readeth let him understand." (Matt. 24 v 15)**

This abomination as Jesus called it is a desecration of the sanctuary of the temple of God. One of the Idols is mentioned as a wing placed on the panicle of the temple and of course the wing was representative of the Roman Empire. The Eagles wing was on their standards or banners.

The forces of the Antichrist will come against Israel and as Jesus said woe unto those that have children at that time. People will flee to the mountains for cover. There will be a terrible attack on the people of Israel by what amounts to the whole world but God has said that the days of tribulation if not stopped would destroy all of His people. So He promised that He will put a stop to it, and the Bible tells us that Jesus will return with a host and destroy the evil from upon Israel.

> **8. "And then shall that wicked be revealed, whom the Lord shall consume with the spirit of his mouth, and shall destroy with the brightness of his coming." (11Thess. 2 v 8)**

Antichrist will be destroyed by the breath and brightness of the Lord, the mere presence of the Lord of hosts will be enough to burn him up and his armies with him.

> **11, "And I saw heaven opened, and behold a white horse; and he that sat upon him was called Faithful and True, and in righteousness he doth judge and make war."**
>
> **12. "His eyes were a flame of fire, and on his head were many crowns; and he had a name written, that no man knew, but he himself."**
>
> **13. "And he was clothed with a vesture dipped in blood: and his name is called The Word of God."**
>
> **14. "And the armies which were in heaven followed him upon white horses, clothed in fine linen, white and clean."**
>
> **15. "And out of his mouth goeth a sharp sword, that with it he should smite the**

nations: and he shall rule them with a rod of Iron: and he treadeth the Winepress of the fierceness and wrath of Almighty God."

16. "And he hath on his vesture and on his thigh a name written KING OF KINGS AND LORD OF LORDS." (Rev. 19 v 11-15)

As the forces of the Antichrist come against Israel, the Bible says they are arrayed against God, showing again in this statement that the Israelis are God's people. Two things are to be considered here. One, Is that the Jews are His people still, and that fighting Israel is fighting against God as far as He's concerned. An association to be considered just as when Jesus told Saul who became Paul, in that He said, "Why persecuteth Me Saul?" In other words He said, "You are persecuting me when you attack the church and Christians". The Church and the Israelis are both equally important to God. The wording implies that as the forces of Antichrist's army are arrayed against Israel, so are the evil forces behind him, the false church and prophet. Those forces are satan and his host of demons, and they are arrayed against the chosen saints and the Angels of God, to do battle at the same time. So this is a battle like there has never been before or ever could have. All the forces both physical and spiritual are fighting at the same time. We can see now why Jesus made that statement about there never being a time like it or ever will be **(Matt. 24 v 21).** Of course evil is totally defeated and eventually thrown into the lake of fire.

In a nutshell what we have is this. We are in a time of dispensation at the moment when we have the opportunity to get as many people as possible saved before the church is taken from the earth. We the church will then be taken up with the Lord for a time as the tribulation starts. The tribulation will begin and for seven years terrible things will be happening on the earth. After this period the Lord will return with a spectacular entrance and save Israel, who is under the most devastating attack the world has ever known.

Once this has occurred the Lord will lock up satan and set up His kingdom on earth for a thousand years. We will at this time be in heaven with the Lord. After which time satan will be released to tempt all those born in that millennium period (1000 yrs). At an appointed time that He knows, those people born in that millennium period that were tempted away, along with all the unsaved people of the world will be brought before the throne of God and the books will be opened and their deeds read out. Another book will be opened called the Lambs book of life and anyone not found in this book will be judged and thrown along with the devil, the Antichrist and the false Prophet, into the lake of fire for eternity. This is White Throne Judgment.

Now some people as I've said, still believe that we have to go through the tribulation that we have to suffer and be tested to see if we are worthy of the Lord and so on. So let's have a look at a few things to clear that up.

> **5. "And God saw that the wickedness of man was great upon the earth and that every imagination of the thoughts of his heart was only evil continually."**
>
> **6. "And it repented the Lord that he had made man on the earth, and it grieved him at his heart." (Gen 6v 6-7)**

The Lord was grieved with His creation in Noah's time and He was going to destroy the evil that men had become. He was really serious about cleaning up the lot of them, but look what happens. The Bible says that "God found grace in the eyes of Noah", **(Gen 6v8)** and decided to get him to build the Ark and put the animals in and so on. Notice what God says in the next chapter;

> **1. "And the Lord said unto Noah, come thou and all thy house into the ark; for thee have I seen righteousness before me in this generation." (Gen. 7v1)**

Notice God spared Noah from the destruction and the physical dangers of the flood; because he saw righteousness in him. In the **eighteenth chapter of Genesis** we find Abraham talking with God, who is about to lower the boom on Sodom. Abraham partitions God on behalf of the people of Sodom saying, if there were fifty righteous men in the city would He spare all. God agrees that if there were fifty righteous people He will spare the town. Abraham then appeals again and eventually after several requests gets God to agree that if there are only ten righteous souls in the city He will spare their city. As it turns out there wasn't so they were destroyed. God did however let Abraham's relative Lot and his wife leave the city.

> **6. "And he believed in the Lord; and he counted it to him for righteousness" (Gen. 15 v 6).**

Here again we see that God's blessing on Abraham was there because God counted his faith and trust in him unto righteousness. Again an example of God sparing and delivering on the basis of righteousness and this time as before with Noah, the blessing was extended to his family. In the book of Daniel we see that Shadrach, Meshach and Abednego were delivered from the fiery furnace and no harm was come to them. **(Dan. 3v 19-25).** Daniel also when thrown into the lion's den was preserved by God who sent an angel to close the mouth of the lions **(Dan. 6v22)**. These men were righteous men before God who honored God and obeyed His word, and their faith in God was justified because God delivered them from evil.

God's whole purpose in sending Jesus was to deliver us from any and everything that is evil and destructive. Why then would people think that God would let those people that Jesus died to make righteous stay on the earth in a hellish situation, when He has told us that we are the righteousness of God in Christ? God does not punish righteousness. The Bible tells us that;

> **6. "And because ye are sons, God hath sent forth the Spirit of his son into your hearts, crying, Abba Father."**
>
> **7. "Wherefore thou art no more a servant but a son; and if a son, then an heir of God through Christ." (Gal. 4 v 6-7)**

It's hard to imagine that God sent the Spirit of His own Son Jesus into our hearts, that's amazing. He then said "you are sons and heirs of God". I know we've been over this a lot already but I just get blown away at the thought of being God's Son through Christ. I really can't imagine God leaving His family in Sodom or to drown in the flood or to be murdered along with crazed Homosexuals as in Lots village. I also can't imagine God leaving His children in the middle of the tribulation. I for one am doing just what Shadrach and the boys did what Noah did, what Daniel did and what Jesus did. I'm going to believe that God wants to and will take me out from the evil coming on this present world.

Again I feel to repeat it;

4. "Who gave himself for our sins, that he might deliver us from this present evil world according to the will of God and our Father" (Gal. 1v4).

At the time that Moses was born there was a law decreed by the Pharaoh of the time that all male Hebrew children should be killed at birth, so as to stop the numbers of the Hebrews escalating so fast. The female children were allowed to live so as they could marry Egyptians and so on. The spiritual implication here as to what was really going on was that satan was trying to breed out the Jewish people so as to stop Christ being born into the earth at a later date. On seeing her baby boy healthy when born Moses mother hid the child for three months from everybody to preserve his life.

God had a plan for Moses before the foundation of the earth just as He has for you and I. Moses' mother inspired by God placed him in a basket lined with pitch and put him in the reeds where Pharaoh's Daughter came to bathe. On finding the baby in the flags she ordered her maid to go and secure someone who could nurse the baby for her, to preserve its life. Well God being God and having a delivering and benefit everybody plan as usual, had her pick Moses' own Mother as the Wet Nurse for the Egyptian woman **(Ex. 2v1-10)**. So not only did God preserve Moses physically but emotionally and spiritually as well, by having him brought up and taught his heritage by his own Mother. He was preserved spiritually, mentally, Physically, Financially, (you do well being paid by Pharaoh in those days and his mother was for wet nursing the child) and socially in that he learned of his own culture and also the ways of the Egyptians.

Again we see God blessing the righteous, a daughter of Abraham, a Jewish woman and her family, preserving them against the tribulation of the times. God always delivers His people whoever they are and at whatever time in history it might be.

When Moses was older God used him to deliver His people, the Jewish nation from the oppression of four hundred years at the hands of the Egyptians. God would have delivered them sooner if they had of cried out to Him earlier.

> 23. "And it came to pass in the process of time that the King of Egypt died: and the children of Israel sighed by reason of their bondage."
>
> 24. "And God heard their groaning, and God remembered His covenant with Abraham, with Isaac, and with Jacob." (Ex. 2v23-24)
>
> 8. "And I am come down to deliver them out of the hand of the Egyptians, and to bring them up out of that land unto a good land and a large, unto a land flowing with milk and honey; unto the place of the Canaanites, and Hittites, and the Amorites, and the Perizzites, and the Hivites, and the Jebusites."
>
> 9. "Now therefore, behold the cry of the children of Israel is come unto me: and I have also seen the oppression wherewith the Egyptians oppress them."
>
> 10. "Come now therefore, and I will send thee to Pharaoh, that thou mayest bring forth my people the children of Israel out of Egypt." (Ex. 3v8-10)

God delivered His people from oppression and the tribulation of Egypt's tyranny. He delivered the individual in Moses' case and

He delivered the Israelis on mass. When He delivered Moses we've already seen that he was delivered completely taken care of, and when He delivered the Children of Israel the Bible says that they were not sick and that they took Pharaoh's people's treasure with them. When they were crossing the desert they were provided for by God in that He gave them warmth at night with a pillar of fire and shelter by day from the sun under a cloud. He provided food in the form of Manner, (Angel food) and quail, and their health was preserved by looking to the serpent on the pole, a type of Christ, or in other words a figure representing the healing that Christ would bring to people when He came in the flesh. The snake representing evil He would save us from.

Just as with Noah, with Lot, with Moses, Shadrach etc. and the Children of Israel themselves, God always delivers and when He does, He does it in such a way that in the deliverance He provides everything we will need for the journey or the transition. Just as He has always done God will deliver us from the tribulation and provide us with everything necessary to be in His presence. The Blood of the Lamb avails for us as we live and breathe, already in place just as His plan for the resurrection of Christ was in place before the crucifixion ever took place.

Notice again that all these scriptures refer to the people as the children. We see ourselves as adults, but God still calls us His children. How many times have you heard a three year old say I'm not little anymore I'm big now? Well we smile and say yes, but we are of the mindset that we will still protect, nurture and love them because they are our children. When they grow and become adults they are grown but in our hearts they are always our Children as we are with God.

Notice this too that when God delivers He doesn't just deliver from, but He always delivers you to something. In the case of the Hebrew Children He delivered them from Egypt to the land of milk and honey. With Lot and Abram He took them to fertile lands to prosper, with Moses it was to a blessed life in Pharaoh's household and with us it will be to a place in paradise away from the tribulation events occurring on the earth.

Another worry for Christians is the speculation and discussion about the Mark of the Beast and just what it may be. Again ask ten people and you'll get ten answers all differing in some way. The

Bible tells us that those on the earth at that time will not be able to buy sell or exchange goods without it. The old movies of the seventies and eighties as I said, portrayed God's people being killed and tortured trying to shop. This was a scare tactic of the times to try and frighten people into the kingdom and prepare others for what they felt was sure martyrdom for those that were alive at the time of the tribulation. Mostly what it did was to scare everybody especially the children. There are people I talk to today as adults that still remember the films that would be shown in Churches on a Sunday night and as a result of which some are still disturbed by the memory of what was projected on to their thoughts. If as they believe you won't be able to buy sell or exchange they wouldn't need to execute you, they could just allow you to starve to death, or die from a lack of medical treatment etc. It will be bad to go through the tribulation but that is a privilege reserved for the Jewish Nation and those that do not get included in the initial catching away of the church.

Most of the Israelis will be destroyed in the end time war but as God has said, "A remnant will be saved" and the number of them will be a hundred and forty four thousand, twelve thousand from each of the tribes of Israel.

A lot of sects' claim that number is relative to them exclusively, two things puzzle me about people like that, one is that the Bible clearly states that that number is relative to the nation of Israel. **Chapter seven of Revelation** explains that, the number is made up from the twelve tribes, twelve thousand from each of the tribes. There are other places also that explain that it is relative to Israel like in **the ninth chapter of Romans verse twenty seven**.

The other thing is that if they believe that only a hundred and forty four thousand of their particular religious sects are going and there are more than one group that hold to that theory and feel that they are the chosen few. After all these years though what makes them think that there is any places left in heaven for them? Surely there would be a 144,000 there by now. Any way that's their business.

Up until a short while ago I always believed the Mark of the beast to be a series of numbers six, six, and six not three sixes but three rows of six numbers, an eighteen digit number which will be our identification number telling the computers that we are who we are, where we live, and whether we are Christians or antichrist worshipers etc. After all we are getting more technically advanced every day it would stand to reason it would be of an advanced technology so people couldn't get around it, but now I'm not so sure. Others believe it to be a brand of some sort like a Roman coin that shows your loyalty to the New Roman Empire or some symbol of the new world order which allows you to operate normally in society. Or at least until the government of the day which will be evil, decides you're toast.

Whatever it is I really don't believe that it is something the Church has to worry about. God will deliver His people as He has always done. Look;

> **3. "Saying hurt not the earth, neither the sea, nor the trees till we have sealed the servants of our God in their foreheads."**
>
> **4. And I heard the number of them which were sealed an hundred and forty and four thousand of all the tribes of the children of Israel." (Rev. 7v3-4)**

The sealing was for the identification as distinct from those who served the beast and took his mark. No reference is made to marking the Church. It just goes on to say that after the Jews are marked John saw a great multitude that no man could number of all the nations and kindreds and people and tongues. They were standing before the throne and before the lamb, clothed with white robes and palms in their hands. **(Rev. 7v9)** Notice, even though it's the remnant going through the tribulation God still does what He can to make sure His people are not caught up in the disastrous events any more than need be. Remember the reason they are going through the tribulation was because they didn't believe on Jesus. The Apostle John saw this vision and wrote down what he saw. He saw the Jews, the remnant, being marked before the earth was ravaged with another calamity so as they were not mixed up with anyone else. But he saw the church the great multitude, standing before the Lamb of God and His throne. We were not with the Jews, nor did he see us involved in anything else at this time of trouble only before the throne worshiping God.

There are many scriptures relating to end times in the Gospels and while we learn from the teachings from the Gospels it is wise to remember as I've said that this is still under the Old Covenant and as such, certain things need to be taken into account at times. In this case for example;

> 26. "And then shall they see the
> Son of man coming in the clouds
> with great power and glory."
>
> 27. "And then shall he send his angels, and shall
> gather together his elect from the four winds,
> from the utter most parts of the earth to the
> uttermost parts of heaven." (Mk. 13 v 26-27)

Here is a scripture that if you don't understand what's going on you might wonder who the elect are. But in the book of **revelation the seventh chapter** relating to Johns vision we just spoke about, he said that the four angels with the four winds should wait and touch not the earth until God had sealed His servants.

God does not call us servants but Sons and Children of God, joint heirs with Christ. This reference is again relative to Israel. At the time this scripture is spoken of and John in his vision was watching it unfold, we were according to his testimony, in the throne room praising God. So again be confident when you read scriptures and warnings of missing out on going to heaven, because a lot of the time Jesus is warning the nation of Israel of their impending tribulation. In this scripture **(Mk. 13v26)** Israel His Elect was on earth watching Him come at the end of the seven years of tribulation. The Church His elect was gathered it says, from the uttermost parts of heaven along with the Angelic host and coming with Him to witness the destruction of the Antichrist armies surrounding Israel.

Once the great battle is over and the thousand year reign is fulfilled and when all things and creatures have been judged. When everything relative to this lifetime has been taken care of: then the Bible says that God will make a new heaven and a new earth. All the old will be folded up and a whole new earth and heavens will be created.

Can you imagine what sort of a day that will be? We will see God create the New Universe.

> 1. "And I saw a new heaven and a new earth: for the first heaven and the first earth were passed away; and there was no more sea."
>
> 2. "And I John saw the Holy City, New Jerusalem, coming down from heaven, prepared as a bride adorned for her husband."
>
> 3. "And I heard a great voice out of heaven saying, behold the tabernacle of God is with men, and he will dwell with them, and they shall be his people, and God himself shall be with them, and be their God."
>
> 4. "And God shall wipe away their tears from their eyes; and there shall be no more death, neither sorrow nor crying, neither shall there be any more pain: for the former things are passed away."
>
> 5. "And he that sat upon the throne said, behold, I make all things new. And he said unto me, write: for these words are true and faithful." (Rev. 21v1-5)

God is so intimately concerned and in love with us that just as after an argument it's good to start afresh with a new attitude and ideas, so too God intends to start a whole New Universe, without tears, without pain and suffering, without conflict, without troubles, without sickness and disease, without hatred, without fornication, without adultery, without wars, without abuse, without loss, without grief, and without the devil, because he caused all that stuff in the first place.

Whether we understand everything that goes on, or how everything is supposed to work out or end, or whether we manage to work out about the mark of the beast or who the Antichrist is and when exactly he will show up, is not as important as it is to live by faith in God's Word. If we live by faith in the Word we will be victorious anyway no matter what happens or when. I for one don't believe as I've said that we will have to go through the tribulation and for that I am grateful to God. I am grateful for everything God has done and is still doing for me. I believe a grateful heart goes a long way to keeping you in the right frame of mind with God, and a Father loves nothing better than to be appreciated by his children. It just makes you as a Father want to do more and more for them all the time and God is no different. Where do you think we Parents get it from? **God's will is to do it for you**

Conclusion

WHAT WE WILL be doing after the new heaven and earth are created is a mystery, but I think, (apart from praising our Loving Heavenly Father), and I've got into trouble for saying this before, but I think like any Father when He has taught us what we need to know, will give us a chance to put that creative force inside us to use and allow us to create things or people of our own to look after; because as any healthy family grows, it produces children which then produce grand children, it's the law of Genesis, everything produces after itself. God having Grandchildren an extended family of children carrying the glory in earthen vessels produced by those that have come through that process, but this time there would be no devil to upset the mix. Now that thought would cause a stir in some circles.

What I do know is this; whatever happens and whatever God has created or is yet to create for those that love Him, it will be the most extraordinarily, beautiful, amazing life in Him for the rest of eternity. We use that word like we really have some grasp as to just how long that is. Never the less it is sure to be a mind blowing experience of Joy and Peace that surpasses anything that we could possible imagine, and I for one am so glad I gave my heart to Jesus Christ when I did. Thank you Jesus for all that you do every day of my life: And for what you will do every day of my life.

Remember**; if it's not total victory total success, it's not God's will for your life** Because, <u>**God's will is to do it for you**</u>.

May God bless you in all you do Amen!

Bibliography

Douglas J. The New Bible Dictionary
Inter-Varsity Press London, 1975.

Jamieson R. Fausset A, Brown D. Commentary on the Whole Bible Zondervan Publishing House Michigan, 1978

Strong, J. Strong's Exhaustive Concordance of the Bible Abingdon Nashville, 1977.

Merriam/Webster Dictionary. Pocket Books New York, 1974.

IF YOU'VE READ this book and you would like to become one of God's children living for ever in peace with Him, say this prayer with a sincerer heart and God will reveal His love to you, save your soul and write your name in the Lambs book of life. You will be part of the blessed resurrection that Jesus talked about, and in the mean time you will be able to communicate with your Heavenly Father and life here will be a lot more joyful.

Father God I come to you now on the basis of your word which says if I come I will not be rejected. I accept Jesus as my Lord and savior and ask that He come into my heart and save my soul. I believe that Jesus died for my sins and was raised from the dead taking death captive and making it possible for me to be reconciled to you my Heavenly Father. I thank you now for saving me and ask that you baptize me in your Holy Spirit and teach me how to live a victorious life in this world. Thank you Lord that I am now your child. Amen.

If you have prayed this prayer I would encourage you to seek out other Christians and tell them of your decision to accept Christ as your savior. You will find that they are happy to meet you even though they don't know you, because they will be pleased to have another brother or sister in the Lord.

A prayer on your behalf

Father I pray for this new family member that you would protect them, teach them and shower their lives with the abundance of love and treasure that is the life in Christ. I pray that the eyes of their understanding be enlightened and that they will grow in the knowledge of you Father and grow daily to become more like Jesus our blessed Lord and Saviour. I thank you Sir for this precious soul and for the privilege of sharing the teaching in this book.

To Contact the Author

If you would like to know more about the author or
The things written in this book we can be contacted at

Robert Albrighton Ministries
P.O. Box 1117 Elizabeth Vale
South Australia 5112
Australia
E-mail: ramharmony1@bigpond.com

When writing please include your testimony or
An acknowledgement of help received
From the teachings in this book.

Also include your prayer requests. We would
Be happy to believe and stand in faith with you.

www.ingramcontent.com/pod-product-compliance
Lightning Source LLC
Chambersburg PA
CBHW030322080526
44584CB00012B/668